Shaping
the Claim

Elements of Preaching
O. Wesley Allen Jr., series editor

Thinking Theologically
The Preacher as Theologian
Ronald J. Allen

Knowing the Context
Frames, Tools, and Signs for Preaching
James R. Nieman

Interpreting the Bible
Exegetical Approaches for Preaching
Mary F. Foskett

Shaping the Claim
Moving from Text to Sermon
Marvin A. McMickle

Determining the Form
Structures for Preaching
O. Wesley Allen Jr.

Finding Language and Imagery
Words for Holy Speech
Jennifer L. Lord

Delivering the Sermon
Voice, Body, and Animation in Proclamation
Teresa L. Fry Brown

Serving the Word
Preaching in Worship
Melinda A. Quivik

Shaping the Claim

Moving from Text to Sermon

Marvin A. McMickle

Fortress Press
Minneapolis

SHAPING THE CLAIM
Moving from Text to Sermon

Cover image: © iStockphoto.com/Igor Skrynnikov
Cover and book design: John Goodman

 Library of Congress Cataloging-in-Publication Data
McMickle, Marvin Andrew.
  Shaping the claim : moving from text to sermon / Marvin A. McMickle.
     p. cm. — (Elements of preaching)
  Includes bibliographical references.
  ISBN 978-0-8006-0429-5 (alk. paper)
  1. Preaching. I. Title.
  BV4211.3.M375 2008
  251—dc22
                        2008024347

Contents

Editor's Foreword   vii

Introduction   1

Chapter 1 • What to Preach?   5
  Logos   5
  What Is a Sermonic Claim?   6
  Sermonic Claims Sunday after Sunday   9
  The Sermonic Claim and the Individual Sermon   18
  From Biblical Text to Sermonic Claim   23
  The Postmodern Challenge   29

Chapter 2 • So What?   33
  Don't Waste a Minute   35
  Pathos   40
  Make It Plain   49
  An Afterword on Patience   51

Chapter 3 • Now What?   55
  Ethos   55
  What Responses Should Preachers Invite?   63
  Balance   73
  How Many Points? Only One   75

Notes   79
Representative Readings   83

Editor's Foreword

Preparing beginning preachers to stand before the body of Christ and proclaim the word of God faithfully, authentically, and effectively Sunday after Sunday is and always has been a daunting responsibility. As North American pastors face pews filled with citizens of a postmodern, post-Christendom culture, this teaching task becomes even more complex. The theological, exegetical, and homiletical skills that preachers need for the future are as much in flux today as they have ever been in Western Christianity. Thus providing seminary students with a solid but flexible homiletical foundation at the start of their careers is a necessity.

Traditionally, professors of preaching choose a primary introductory textbook that presents a theology of proclamation and a process of sermon development and delivery from a single point of view. To maintain such a singular point of view is the sign of good writing, but it does at times cause problems for learning in pluralistic settings. One approach to preaching does not fit all. Yet a course simply surveying all of the homiletical possibilities available will not provide a foundation on which to build either.

Furthermore, while there are numerous introductory preaching textbooks from which to choose, most are written from the perspective of Euro-American males. Classes supplement this view with smaller homiletical texts written by women and persons of color. But a pedagogical hierarchy is nevertheless set up: the white male voice provides the main course and women and persons of color provide the side dishes.

Elements of Preaching is a series designed to help professors and students of preaching—including established preachers who want to develop their skills in specific areas—construct a sound homiletical foundation in a conversational manner. This conversation is meant to occur at two levels. First, the series as a whole deals with basic components found in most introductory preaching classes: theology of proclamation, homiletical contexts, biblical interpretation, sermonic claim, language and imagery, rhetorical form, delivery, and worship. But each element is presented by a different scholar, all of whom represent diversity in terms of gender, theological traditions (Baptist, Disciple of Christ, Lutheran, Presbyterian, and United Methodist), and ethnicity (African American, Asian American, and Euro-American). Instead of bringing in different voices at the margin of the preaching class, Elements of Preaching creates a conversation around the central topics of an introductory course without foregoing essential instruction concerning sermon construction and embodiment. Indeed, this level of conversation is extended beyond the printed volumes through the Web site www.ElementsofPreaching.com.

Second, the individual volumes are written in an open-ended manner. The individual author's particular views are offered but in a way that invites, indeed demands, the readers to move beyond them in developing their own approaches to the preaching task. The volumes offer theoretical and practical insights, but at the last page it is clear that more must be said. Professors and students have a solid place to begin, but there is flexibility within the class (and after the class in ministry) to move beyond these volumes by building on the insights and advice they offer.

In this volume, Marvin A. McMickle discusses the development of the sermonic claim. By "sermonic claim" McMickle means that central focus and intent of the preacher which is aimed at claiming the hearers at the deepest existential level possible. Preachers too often spend hour upon hour on exegetically determining what a biblical text says only to rush through the determination of what they want to say to get to the task of spending hour upon hour determining how to say it (in terms of developing imagery and a sermonic form). McMickle invites us to slow down and ponder three aspects of developing a claim. Drawing on Aristotle's categorization of types of persuasion—*logos, pathos,* and *ethos*—he shows how for every sermon a preacher must decide what to say, how to engage the emotions, and what behavior to inspire. In other words, this book helps preachers determine what they want a congregation to think, feel, and do during and in response to the sermonic event. By giving attention to the elemental task of developing a clear, relevant sermonic claim in the manner McMickle proposes, preachers will find their sermons moving beyond an expository lecture or self-help motivational speech to an authentic expression of the good news of Jesus Christ that has an impact on those gathered before the Word.

O. Wesley Allen Jr.

Introduction

During my years as a student at Union Theological Seminary in the City of New York, I developed a deep interest in the work of biblical exegesis, hermeneutics, and the work that is involved in making the shift from the critical study of Scripture to the preparation and delivery of sermons. That interest led me temporarily into a Ph.D. program in Old Testament at Columbia University, but eventually into a career as a pastor for the past thirty-three years and a teacher of homiletics for the past twenty-five years. While there have been many career shifts and changes in locale along the way, one thing has remained constant: a deep interest in the shift from the work of biblical exegesis to the work of sermon design and delivery.

My first published attempt to give expression to this lifelong interest came with my 2001 volume, *Living Water for Thirsty Souls: Unleashing the Power of Exegetical Preaching* (Judson Press). I am excited about the prospects of continuing to examine the process of moving from text to sermon with this Elements of Preaching volume from Fortress Press. I am deeply committed to the concept of biblical preaching regardless of the sermon form that might be employed. Whether one is engaged in expository, doctrinal, topical, dialectic, narrative, biographical, or inductive/deductive forms of preaching, I believe that preaching is best done when the sermon rests upon the insights and authority of a biblical text. How to bridge the gap between the end of the process of exegesis and the preparation and delivery of the sermon is what this volume has set out to examine.

This book will be broken into three chapters, each of which will examine a different aspect of the process of shaping the basic claim or the central theme or message of the sermon. The first chapter will ask the question "What to preach?" and will examine how preachers can arrive at a basic theme or message around which their sermon can be built. The second chapter will ask the question "So what?" and will seek to make the point that solid content alone is not enough if the sermon does not make an almost immediate existential/experiential connection with the listeners. The third chapter will raise the question

"Now what?" and will remind preachers that sermons are not complete until they have pointed the listeners to some appropriate next steps that should be taken as a result of having heard that sermon.

Each of those three chapters will be informed by the three goals offered by Aristotle in his reflections on rhetoric; *logos, pathos,* and *ethos.* The chapter on "What to preach?" will reflect on Aristotle's use of the word *logos* and will make the case that every sermon must be based upon a clear and compelling claim that is rooted in Scripture and that is culturally relevant for the audience to which it is being directed. The chapter on "So what?" will draw from Aristotle's understanding of *pathos* and will make the case that sermons must be preached with passion and enthusiasm, and must also seek to ignite passion and enthusiasm in those who hear the message. Finally, the chapter on "Now what?" will use Aristotle's concept of *ethos* to imagine the kinds of next steps that listeners might take as a result of having heard the word of the Lord. Sermons are not simply to be heard; they are to create some response on the part of those who have heard.

I am deeply indebted to several people who first ignited my interest in this critical juncture in the preaching process. First, I acknowledge my indebtedness to Dr. James A. Sanders, who remains the best Bible scholar I have ever encountered. His lectures on the Old Testament were delivered with the precision of a classical scholar but also with the fervor of a southern revivalist. It was a joy to watch him at work, and I am certain that his influence on my life and thought continues to this day. So far as preaching influences are concerned, I was blessed to be alive and in my formative years as a preacher in New York City when Samuel Proctor, Gardner Taylor, William A. Jones, Sandy Ray, Ernest Campbell, David H. C. Read, and William Sloane Coffin were preaching in that city. I can think of no time in American history when I would rather have been alive so far as it concerns the richness of the pulpits of New York City.

Week after week for five wonderful years, I was able to wander that great city and observe these master preachers at work. They were doing the very thing I have been trying to understand—solid biblical exegesis resulting in solid sermon content that challenged the mind, filled the soul, and lifted the spirit to heights sublime. How did they accomplish that affect? What were their devices, their techniques, their styles of sermon design and delivery? Those were the questions

I was asking then. Those are the answers I have been pursuing for twenty-five years as a teacher of preaching. Those are the questions that hovered over me as I wrote this book.

I am equally grateful to Dr. Fred Finks, who was the President at Ashland Theological Seminary when I was hired there as a professor of preaching. It was my belief that I would do my best work as a teacher of preaching if I could remain actively involved in pastoral ministry and the weekly task of preaching to the same congregation. Not every seminary president would agree to such an arrangement, and not every professor of preaching feels as I do about maintaining this balance between the classroom and the local church. He was willing to take a chance on such an arrangement, however, and I have worked hard since he hired me in 1996 to live up to his trust and confidence. The members of Antioch Baptist Church of Cleveland, Ohio, hold an equally cherished place in my heart. They, too, agreed to this shared ministry between themselves and the seminary. I have been with them since 1987, and our friendship and partnership in the service of Jesus Christ only deepens as the years go by.

I am thankful to Fortress Press for the chance to be a part of this series of books that grapples with various aspects of the preaching task. It is an honor to be associated with the men and women whose volumes will comprise this series. It has been a special delight to work with O. Wesley Allen who not only drafted me to be a part of this project, but who then offered editorial assistance that was so expert that there were times I could not tell where my words ended and his suggested changes began. He deserves immense credit for any compliments this book may receive. Any shortcomings and failures belong entirely to me.

Chapter 1

What to Preach?

In the beginning was the Word . . . —John 1:1

Logos

The first passage of Scripture I ever translated from Greek to English over forty years ago when I was still a college student was the prologue to the Gospel of John. The opening line in 1:1 reads, *En archē ēn ho logos*, which translates into, "In the beginning was the Word." After all of these years, that phrase continues to echo and resound in my heart—"In the beginning was the Word." I begin this book where John began his Gospel, where all preachers should begin their sermon preparation—in the beginning must be the Word.

Every sermon should be focused upon a specific message or lesson that is anchored in Scripture and transmitted to a congregation. That is the use of "the word" as spelled with a lowercase "w"—a word *from* God. In Scripture there are a multitude of such "words." However, sermons should also be centered upon "the Word," spelled with an uppercase "W." Christian sermons should be centered in the person and work of Jesus Christ—who is the Word *of* God. Sermons should speak of Christ, elevate Christ, and point people to the teachings and blessings that reside in Christ. In sermons, therefore, preachers bring together a different word each week and the unchanging Word that is worshiped week after week.

5

The use of the word *logos* ("word") in John 1:1 calls to mind Aristotle's use of the same Greek word in his discussion on rhetoric where he talks about *logos, pathos,* and *ethos.*[1] A shorthand version of Aristotle's approach to rhetoric or public speaking would state, first, that when we stand to speak we need to have something to say that is worth saying (*logos*). Second, if it is worth saying, then it is worth saying well (*pathos*). Third, it does not matter how well something of importance is said if the person doing the talking is not a person of integrity whose conduct contradicts the message being declared (*ethos*).

In Greek, *logos* can have a range of nuances—word, logic, rationale, or idea. When the terminology of Aristotle is translated into the terminology of this study, the word *logos* represents the content or claim of the sermon. *Logos* constitutes what the sermon is about. That is the equivalent of the question, "What to preach?" which will be central to this chapter. In the second and third chapters, we will pay attention to Aristotle's treatment of *pathos* and *ethos.* But for now we begin where John and Aristotle begin: with the word of the sermon.

What Is a Sermonic Claim?

The phrase "sermonic claim" is meant to imply that a sermon ought to do one of the following things: assert something that is significant, ask for something that is substantial to the point requiring personal or communal commitment, or advocate for something that is sacred and deeply spiritual. Let me set forth a description of preaching that seeks to focus on this idea of a sermonic claim:

> Every sermon needs to make *one* clear, compelling, biblically centered, and contextually relevant claim that sets some aspect of God's will and God's word before some specific segment of God's people. This is done with the hope that those people will be challenged, informed, corrected, or encouraged as a result of the word set before them that day.

Plainly stated, the sermonic claim is the essence of what any sermon is about. It is the central truth or teaching of that sermon. It is a creative and engaging combination of what the biblical text says, how that message is communicated by the preacher, and some direction as regards what the listeners are being asked to do as a result of hearing that sermon. What is being referred to here as the sermonic claim has been discussed and/or defined by other teachers of homiletics as well as by leading preachers who consider this idea of the sermon being focused on "one clear, compelling, biblically centered, and contextually relevant claim." Haddon Robinson calls it "the main point or the big idea of the sermon."[2] Samuel Proctor calls it "the proposition or the relevant question."[3] What we are holding together in the phrase "sermonic claim"—what the sermon says and what the sermon is intended to do—Thomas G. Long discusses in terms of the "focus" and "function" of the sermon.[4]

Fred Craddock is especially helpful when he refers to this idea of a sermonic claim as "the theme" of the sermon that the preacher should be able to state in one simple sentence. He reminds the preacher that in shaping a sermon one is not only determining what *will* be said in that sermon, one is also deciding what *will not* be said, at least not in that sermon. Craddock helpfully warns the preacher that the biblical text(s) we use for a sermon may hold more than one significant message that could be usefully explored and examined. It is rare that any one sermon can be shaped so that it allows all of that material and all of those possible insights to be covered.[5] That is where the sermonic claim comes in; it helps sort through all of the things that *could* be said in any one sermon, and helps to narrow the preacher's focus down to what *should* and *will* be said in this particular sermon. As Craddock points out, there is a benefit for both the preacher and the congregation when the sermon has a single focus. He says: "To aim at nothing is to miss everything, but to be specific and clear in one's presentation is to make direct contact with many whose ages, circumstances, and apparent needs are widely divergent. Listeners to sharply focused sermons have an amazing capacity to perceive that the sermon was prepared with them specifically in mind."[6]

The sermonic claim is not one of the many parts of the sermon. It is the basic assertion that is being made in the sermon. In fact, all of the parts of the sermon should be coordinated so that they all support, and in no way conflict with or obscure that basic assertion. Every sermon will undoubtedly have multiple parts or sections, such as an introduction, imagery, applications, and a conclusion. However, each of these components is important only insofar as they serve a common purpose, specifically helping listeners focus on the sermonic claim.

The introduction should be interesting to the point of being intriguing, but its true value is in its setting the sermon in context for the major claim that is about to be stated. Imagery is not meant to be an anecdotal diversion from the main theme of the sermon. Rather, it should serve to bring clarity and a keener comprehension of the point set forth in the sermonic claim. Applications are the places in the sermon when the relevance of the sermonic claim is being made to those who are hearing the sermon. They demonstrate why it is important that people listen to and act upon what they are hearing in the sermon. Conclusions are not simply meant to bring the sermon to an end. Rather, the conclusion is meant to refocus attention on the central sermonic claim that has just been explored, and then hint at or clearly state what the preacher hopes the listeners will do as a result of having heard the sermon. All elements of the sermon should flow out of and be in service to a singular sermonic claim.

While it may sound simple to write out a simple, declarative sentence that will focus the content of the sermon, the task is quite difficult, given the responsibility of the preacher to bring together a word with the Word. Sermons should spring up from and bear forth the great themes embedded in the Scriptures—justice, grace, the sovereignty of God, the divinity of Christ, the sinful nature of humanity, discipleship, stewardship, the authority of Scripture, and the work of missions and evangelism throughout the world. Sermons should emerge from the heart-wrenching questions and concerns that reside within the congregation and within the life of the preacher as well. Sermons should help people bridge the gap between the faith they hold dear and the troubling events they hear about in the news.

The sermonic claim we develop must challenge people concerning things that are important to their faith and to their lives. It should not be based upon things that do not matter as people are attempting to navigate their way through life. It should not engage things that are irrelevant or inconsequential. Preachers should always try to deal with things that can make a serious, positive difference in the lives of those who hear your sermons, the church in which they gather, and the world in which they live.

When I was growing up in Chicago, Illinois, in the 1950s and 1960s, it was not uncommon to hear one person insult or criticize another with the phrase, "He/she ain't about nothing." There was no more dismissive or demeaning statement that one person could direct against another than to say this to the person. To say this meant that the person in question was not worthy of much attention and should not be expected to produce much in the way of accomplishment. "He/she ain't about nothing" suggested that the person in question should not be taken seriously or expected to have anything significant to contribute to any discussion or the resolution of any problem. Too many sermons on too many Sundays "ain't about nothing." Too many sermons are limited to superficial or simplistic considerations that make no real difference or have no substantive bearing on the great issues of life.

Sermons ought to be about things that are biblically and theologically compelling. Sermons ought to be about things that are intellectually challenging and engaging. Sermons ought to be about things that are contextually and personally relevant and applicable to the lives of those who hear the word on any given day.

Sermonic Claims Sunday after Sunday

If every sermon ought to have a biblically centered message that is culturally relevant and designed to challenge, inform, or encourage those who hear them, then the next issue that needs to be addressed is how preachers can efficiently arrive at preaching material that meets that goal. Preachers need to establish some system or methodology for text and topic selection. Such a system allows the preacher to move quickly from the open-ended question, "What to preach?" in general to the more compelling question of what to say regarding the specific biblical text or preaching topic that has been selected or assigned.

Choosing your approach needs to be more than following your hunches from week to week or hoping for some news that can get your creative juices flowing. While you should be able to adjust to major events when they occur, such events will likely not occur every week. Without a reliable system the likelihood is that preachers will operate within too narrow a field of texts and topics, within their theological, pastoral, or ethical comfort zone. Only some systematic approach to text and topic selection can rescue preaching from that trap. There are several systems that can be employed either as a preacher's sole approach to text and topic selection, or as they are interspersed with one another over the course of a year's preaching in order to have the greatest chance of "proclaiming the whole will of God" (Acts 20:27).

The Lectionary

The first method of text and topic selection that will be discussed when a preacher is considering what to preach next is the Revised Common Lectionary. The lectionary is a list of predetermined texts for each Sunday taken from the Old Testament, the Psalter, the Gospels, and the New Testament (usually an epistle) for three cycles through the liturgical year (Advent, Christmas, Sundays after Epiphany, Lent, Easter, and the Sundays after Pentecost). It leads the preacher in a journey across the canon. The lectionary is a reminder to preachers that the Bible consists of sixty-six books with a wide array of literary genres or types, and the search for preaching material should not be limited to those with which the preacher is most familiar or most comfortable. Pastors should be willing to examine and preach from every area of the canon. Preachers who are comfortable with preaching on Romans will be invited to consider the content of Ruth and Revelation as well. The Revised Common Lectionary will take preachers into passages and preaching topics they would never have considered or would never have been considered.

While the most immediate benefit of the lectionary is the balance it brings to the work of the preacher, there is another great benefit as well. You cannot underestimate or undervalue the time the lectionary saves those preachers who face every Monday morning with the agonizing question of what to do next Sunday. That step has already been covered by these preassigned readings. The preacher is now free to devote maximum time to the larger and more substantive question of what to say about any one or all of those four texts. Instead of the harried search for a text or a topic for next week, the preacher who follows the lectionary can get down to the hard work of preparing "one clear, compelling, biblically centered, culturally relevant claim that sets some aspect of God's word before some specific segment of God's people."

In fairness, there are some preachers who have cautioned against too great a dependence upon the lectionary, believing that by following a preselected group of texts the preacher is robbed of both creativity and spontaneity in the search for relevant preaching material. For example, Ernest Campbell, a preacher and teacher of great note, has written that "the aim of the lectionary is coverage whereas the aim of preaching ought to be relevance.[7] He worries that when the preacher is locked into a blind adherence to an assigned text from week to week, the preacher may miss a "teachable moment" if and when some unexpected event should occur that might open up a wonderful opportunity for creative preaching.[8] Let me set forth several other methods for text and topic selection that will assist preachers in quickly deciding what to preach and what sermonic claim to make without losing spontaneity or creativity.

Following the Liturgical Calendar

Even though the lectionary is closely related to the liturgical calendar, one may follow the doctrinal and seasonal themes associated with the church year without using the lectionary. The thematically focused seasons extend from Advent through Pentecost.

Advent includes the four Sundays prior to Christmas. During this season, the sermons can focus on texts in Micah or Isaiah that anticipated the coming of the Messiah and how the Gospel writers linked the birth of Christ to that expectation. Attention can also be given to texts in Acts and 1 Thessalonians that look ahead to the second coming of Christ as well.

The liturgical emphasis moves next to *Christmas* and the doctrine of the incarnation of God in Jesus Christ. That season of preaching should not be limited to the familiar passages in Matthew and Luke that take us to Bethlehem and to the manger and the shepherds. Christmas is also a time to consider the prologue in John 1:1-14 and Paul's only apparent reference to the birth of Christ found in Galatians 4:4.

The last day of Christmastide is *Epiphany*, the time when the story about Christ first being revealed to the three Magi is now shared throughout the world. The Sundays that follow Epiphany would do well to focus on evangelism and global ministry, as well as issues dealing with God's sovereignty over the whole of creation. In addition to the primary Epiphany text in Matthew 2:1-12, texts such as John 4, about the Samaritan woman who tells her village about Christ, and Acts 8, where an Ethiopian eunuch carries the message back to his home country, can be considered.

The mood shifts dramatically when Lent arrives and the church is invited into a season of introspection. *Lent* begins on Ash Wednesday, which is followed by seven weeks focused on issues of self-examination, the sinful nature of humanity, our need for salvation, and themes of fasting and self-denial as spiritual disciplines that can draw us closer to God. Lent is not simply giving up some favorite food for forty or fifty days and then going right back to it after Easter. Instead, Lent invites the listeners to take some of the time they have freed up as a result of their fasting to focus on some of the spiritual disciplines they may have been ignoring, such as prayer, Bible study, meditation, and self-examination of one's soul and of one's relationship with God. The Psalms and the way they focus prayer and spirituality in many directions can be especially helpful for preaching during this season of the year.

The next stop on the liturgical calendar is *Holy Week* and the themes that run from the triumphal entrance of Jesus into Jerusalem on Palm Sunday through the crucifixion of Christ on the cross as the atonement for the sins of the world. Of course, there is much that takes place between those two events that might become the focus of preaching throughout the week.

Lent and Holy Week give way to the *season of Easter,* which is called the Great Fifty Days, extending from Easter Sunday to Pentecost. On Easter Sunday we can preach not only on the stories of the empty tomb but also on theological reflection on the resurrection, such as is found in 1 Corinthians 15. And the celebration of the resurrection need not be a one-day event. The implications of the resurrection and God's victory over death can be considered throughout Eastertide. The Sundays following Easter are marvelous opportunities to preach on such issues as what we believe about life after death, God's power that extends even to the grave, the question of faith in the face of the mystery of resurrection, and the many other wonders and miracles mentioned in the Bible. Such themes lead well into *Pentecost* and the celebration of the birth of the Christian church as reported in Acts 2. This celebration can be followed with several Sundays used to cover the many themes that emerge as a result of Pentecost. There is the doctrine of the Trinity and the role and work of the Holy Spirit (Trinity Sunday is the first Sunday after Pentecost). There is the unique issue of the outpouring of the Holy Spirit on the disciples and the issue of speaking in tongues or glossolalia that is of such great importance to many in the Pentecostal and charismatic communities. It also points to the multinational composition of that first congregation versus the homogeneous composition of most contemporary churches. Finally, it forces us to consider the communal life that was established among those early believers, and how that compares and contrasts with how we in the modern church care for and share with one another.

Lectio Continua

Any discussion of preaching that touches upon the use of the lectionary or following the liturgical calendar should be followed by a brief reference to an approach to preaching, popularized by preachers of the Reformation era, called *lectio continua*, which simply means preaching straight through all or some significant portion of the Bible. Harold T. Bryson helpfully observes that "To preach *from* a book is different than preaching *through* a book. . . . To *cover* a book is to preach extensively from it. *Coverage* means to select texts and topics."[9] *Lectio continua* invites preachers to adopt this more expository approach to preaching and simply preach from one verse to the next; from one chapter to the next; from one book to the next; from the Old Testament straight into the New Testament; without leaving out or skipping over any troublesome passage along the way.

One might want to begin the use of *lectio continua* with a less ambitious goal than preaching through the entire Bible. Preaching through one of the Old Testament prophets or through one of the Gospels might be a good place to start. The same could be said for preaching through one of the epistles of Paul, Peter, or John. The *lectio continua* approach runs the risk of becoming tedious if the preacher returns the listeners to the same biblical material for too many weeks in a row. The preacher must take care when using this approach to be sure that each sermon in a long series is a fresh contribution and not just a restatement of material being rehashed over and over again. Bryson is helpful at this point as well when he observes, "The audience does not need to be brought up to date on previous sermons in the series. Each sermon should be designed for that particular day."[10]

Another way to use the *lectio continua* approach to preaching is to place a limit on how many weeks or months one will employ this approach before switching to some other method of text and topic selection. One leading proponent of this approach to preaching is Hughes Oliphant Old, who became persuaded about the use of *lectio continua* by reviewing the preaching of John Calvin and Ulrich Zwingli. Remembering that the Reformers and many more contemporary preachers like Donald Barnhouse, Charles Spurgeon, or John R. W.

Stott might spend years preaching through some continuous section of Scripture, it is useful to hear Old state that in his own approach to preaching "I rarely preach more than a dozen sermons on a book in a series."[11]

It should also be remembered that many of the reformers preached every day, unlike most contemporary preachers that might preach only once or twice each week. Calvin and Zwingli could accomplish in one week what could take us two months to accomplish. Nevertheless, despite the need to give careful attention to how long one might want to follow this approach to preaching there is great benefit in making occasional use of the *lectio continua* approach to preaching.

Preaching and the National Calendar

In addition to following the liturgical calendar, the claims made by our sermons can be informed by the themes and observances that flow out of the major holidays and special emphases associated with the national calendar of events. Preachers can appropriate secular celebration as occasions to make a Christ-centered claim. The minds of most people are already open to the themes and topics for those special days, and the preacher can help to sharpen and even shape the focus.

However, preachers who relate sermons to national celebrations need to beware the possibility of drifting into a form of civil religion so well described by Robert Bellah and others,[12] and so blatantly employed by many televangelists in recent years who invented the term "patriot pastors."[13] American patriotism and Christian piety are not synonymous terms. National holidays can be a good time to point out the differences between the Christian faith and contemporary American political maneuvering. As an editorial in *Christianity Today* stated: "George W. Bush is not God. The Declaration of Independence is not an infallible guide to Christian faith and practice. . . . The American flag is not the cross. The Pledge of Allegiance is not the creed. God bless America is not the doxology."[14] The idea of speaking truth to power is an appropriate way to shape a sermonic claim in relation to the national calendar. God is the sovereign of the whole creation and wants to bless all the nations of the earth, not just America.

Let's consider some of the major holidays to which sermons can relate.[15]

The secular calendar begins on January 1 with *New Year's Day*. This celebration allows for an opportunity to consider innumerable topics such as unfinished business, new beginnings, time is marching on, we have come this far by faith, and being willing to walk by faith and not by sight into an uncertain future.

Martin Luther King Jr. Day, the third Monday in January, is a wonderful opportunity to explore themes related to King's concerns about racism, poverty, militarism, and violence. King ceased to be only a civil rights leader, and became a cutting-edge social critic when he began discussing the redistribution of wealth in America and called for the Poor People's Campaign in Washington, D.C., in 1968. His advocacy for the garbage workers in Memphis, Tennessee, was as much about economics as it was about race. His opposition to the Vietnam War was driven by his opposition to violence on the one hand, and by his belief that the money spent to fight the war in Southeast Asia would have been better spent fighting the War on Poverty that President Lyndon Johnson had declared in 1965.

While *Valentine's Day* (February 14) is traditionally celebrated with candy and flowers, preachers should not hand this day or the definition of love over to advertisers and merchandisers. *Love* is a word we should fight to redefine according to biblical principles. On the Sunday nearest Valentine's, a sermon could shift the discussion from *eros*, or the emotional and sentimental passions shared by lovers, to the more demanding forms of love revealed in the Greek language, such as *phileo* that challenges us to love and care for our neighbors, and *agape* that points us to that self-sacrificing form of love that God revealed on the cross with Jesus.

Memorial Day (the last Monday in May) offers a range of pastoral issues worth considering in the pulpit: death, grief, loneliness, and longing for those we have loved and lost. The holiday allows us to remember not only those who have been killed in one of our nation's wars but also anyone killed in the line of duty—police officers, firefighters, paramedics—as well as family and friends who have died. Moreover, the day's focus reminds us of our own mortality. Preachers who lift up these themes at times other than at funerals empower congregants to better sustain themselves when the death of a loved one rolls around.

Independence Day (the Fourth of July) is rich with possible sermonic claims about the nature of freedom, the role and authority of government, the constant threat of tyranny that endangers democracy, the equal worth of every person, and a reminder that freedom and liberty are often purchased and maintained at a very high cost in human suffering and sacrifice. One might also shape a sermonic claim around freedom in Christ and God's sovereignty over our country and world.

Labor Day is celebrated on the first Monday in September and lifts up themes that link the dignity of human labor with receiving a fair wage for one's efforts. With jobs in the United States being outsourced increasingly, with the shift in the economy from a manufacturing-based world to an information-based world, Labor Day allows many angles from which several important issues can be considered. What about a "living-wage ordinance" for our public employees? What are the implications of unionization in a world where nonunionized Wal-Mart is the single largest employer? How do Christians who believe in the sovereignty of God respond to the fact that most products once made in the United States are now made in China, and most service jobs once performed in the United States are now being performed in India?

Columbus Day (second Monday in October) and *St. Patrick's Day* (March 17) provide preachers with an opportunity to focus on issues of ethnic pride on the one hand and issues of racial and ethnic intolerance on the other hand. Columbus Day reminds us of the events of 1492 and the arrival of Europeans into the New World of the Americas. For all of the courage and valor of the explorers who risked their lives to make that voyage, the story also includes glimpses into human sin marked by greed for gold and the genocide that eventually consumed millions of Native Americans from Canada to Chile and from Hawaii to Hispaniola.

Veterans' Day (November 11) is a good time to honor those who served during one of our nation's war as well as those who served during peacetime. It is a time to remember the human and financial costs of war and to ask ourselves whether that is how God wants to see us expend our resources. It is a time to ask about the very nature of war in a world that is marked by nationless terrorist groups, unstable political regimes that have access to nuclear weapons, and about the eschatological vision of both Micah 4:3 and Isaiah 2:4 of a day when nations will "beat their swords into plowshares, and their spears into pruning hooks, . . . and study war no more."

Thanksgiving Day (fourth Thursday in November) very nearly speaks for itself as we pause to focus on the manifold blessings that God has bestowed upon this country. On the one hand, preachers could take a "count your blessings" approach, reminding hearers of the many reasons we all have to give thanks. On the other hand, the sermon could also shift from giving thanks to giving to others in response to how much has been given to us.

Preaching a Rotation of Doctrinal and Theological Themes

The question, "What to preach?" requires that special attention be given to the role of doctrinal preaching. For the last half-century, preachers and scholars have focused on the importance of including doctrine as a required part of the preacher's schedule. An earlier generation of preachers would have been familiar with the work of the British New Testament scholar, C. H. Dodd, who observed that the preaching of the early church focused largely on a body of teachings or doctrines called the *kerygma* (Greek for "proclamation").[16] Included in those doctrines that were meant to be shared with or announced to the world were a group of theological themes deemed essential for a person who desired to have a comprehensive understanding of the Christian faith. These included the doctrines of incarnation (God was in Christ), the mission and ministry of Jesus (the things Jesus said and did), the suffering and death of Christ (the work of atonement and redemption on the cross of Calvary), the resurrection of Christ from the dead, the mission and ministry of the church in the world as witnesses (*marturias* in the Greek or "martyrs for Christ" in Acts 1:8), and the eschatological end of time or the second coming of Christ.

Such doctrinal preaching was abandoned for awhile, but recently, some scholars of various theological orientations have argued for the explication of theology in the pulpit once again.[17] As Robert Smith Jr., in his book *Doctrine That Dances*, states:

> While doctrine may exist to make preaching as disciplined as it needs to be, doctrine's mission is to be a servant to proclamation. Doctrine's purpose is not merely to be derived, constructed, and formalized and to remain in the

archives of academia for scholarly use only. Rather, doctrine is the posses-
sion of the church and must be preached. Preaching extracts its commu-
nicative strength from the reservoirs of doctrine and draws its riches from
the wells of its truths. The doctrine behind and below the sermon gives it
stability.[18]

In an age marked by unfamiliarity with biblical content, it is equally
likely that the average churchgoer has little if any familiarity with the
basic doctrinal and theological beliefs of the Christian faith. Preachers
can do much to address and resolve this problem by systematically
working through themes such as these either during some set period
of time during the year or interspersed over the course of a year's
preaching. The easiest way to begin is to give some attention to the
doctrinal traditions of your denomination/tradition.

The Sermonic Claim and the Individual Sermon

Having a system for planning sermons from Sunday to Sunday will
save preachers time each week as they begin the sermon-preparation
process. But the process of actually beginning to develop a sermonic
claim for each particular sermon still needs further discussion. There
are a number of possible starting points.

Starting with the Bible

Because preachers aim to offer congregations a "biblically centered
and contextually relevant" word, sermon preparation often begins
with a text. Preachers will never have to worry about what to preach
when they begin by giving consideration to the rich resources of biblical material—a reservoir of preaching that speaks to every imagin-
able aspect of human experience awaits any preacher who develops
a systematic way of looking directly to the Bible for the claims and
content of their sermons. Preachers should look and listen closely to
the teachings, parables, doctrines, prophetic oracles, human encoun-
ters, miraculous moments, and character flaws and foibles so candidly
and honestly revealed in the lives of characters recorded in the Bible.
There are lessons to be learned in the Bible about the divine-human
encounter and about the struggle of living godly lives in a sinful world.
The Bible talks about a God who can sustain and deliver people who
are facing hopeless and desperate situations. It deals with issues of

immigration and the mass movement of populations of people. One cannot read about the story of Israel that begins with "a wandering Aramean" and continues with them being an essentially migrant or nomadic population and not see the connection it establishes with the millions of people in our world today who have chosen or been forced to become migrants. The Bible addresses oppression and war and as such can speak to the personal, national, and international cost of such violence. The Bible does not shy away from issues of racial prejudice, and as such it has much to say to a society still deeply divided by race and ethnicity born out of hundreds of years of African slavery, the exploitation and destruction of Native Americans, and/or the recent rise of anti-Islamic sentiment.

A sermonic claim can emerge when a preacher looks and listens to the Scriptures for questions and answers that mirror and shed light on twenty-first-century concerns, issues, and events. Preachers would do well to look to Scripture as the most regular and reliable source of preaching material. It will not take long before the issue of what to preach moves from not knowing *where to look* for a sermon idea, to not knowing *what to do* with all the ideas that can emerge out of the careful review of any passage of Scripture.

While the movement for sermon preparation is usually from "biblically centered" to "culturally relevant," it can go in the opposite direction. The following options explore this movement.

Starting with the Drama of Human Life

The sermonic claim can arise out of the heart-wrenching questions that reside within the life of the congregation, including the life of the preacher. Is there really life after death? Why did I contract HIV, cancer, or some other life-threatening disease when I have been living a good, Christian life? How do I redefine my worth and my identity now that I have lost my job as a result of downsizing or corporate takeovers, or lost my breast as a result of a mastectomy? If I get a divorce from an abusive spouse, can I remarry without being considered an adulterer? What should I do if my children do not choose to embrace this Christian faith that has meant so much to me?

While it is possible that questions such as these could be addressed when the preacher begins with the biblical text and looks for points of application, what is being suggested here is that sometimes the preacher can start with these emotional questions and concerns and then connect them to a biblical text that faithfully addresses the issues at hand. Frankly, this is how most people who hear our sermons come to the Scriptures. They are led there by their pain and their problems. There is some trial or trouble already at work in their lives and they wonder if the Bible in particular and the Christian faith in general can provide them with any assistance or direction.

This approach to preaching is as old as Jeremiah 37:17, where King Zedekiah is facing the possible conquest of his nation by the Babylonians and is in search of some direction. He brings Jeremiah from his imprisonment in a dungeon into the king's palace and asks him, "Is there any word from the LORD?" The same phenomenon is as true for us in the twenty-first century c.e. as it was for Zedekiah in the seventh century b.c.e. People come to worship with all their troubles and worries, asking, "Is there any word from the Lord?" Pastors will have an insider's knowledge of some of the deeply troubling questions and concerns alive within their congregation. All of their real-life questions can be the starting point for a sermon as the preacher searches the Scriptures for guidance, correction, or assurance for people who are caught up in the trials and temptations of daily life.

Haddon Robinson speaks to this approach to preaching in his classic book, *Biblical Preaching*, in which he says:

> The expositor must also be aware of the currents swirling across his [sic] own times, for each generation develops out of its own history and culture and speaks its own language. A minister may stand before a congregation and deliver exegetically accurate sermons, scholarly and organized, but dead and powerless because they ignore the life-wrenching problems and questions of the hearers.[19]

Starting with Current Events
Another source of preaching material arises from the headlines of the morning newspapers. There is concern about the war on terror, upcoming elections, climate change, the spread of highly contagious diseases, and the millions of people who may have to face that reality without medical insurance. There are regular reports of terrorist attacks, fears about illegal immigration, deep concerns about the shifting composition of the U.S. Supreme Court and what that means for

women's reproductive rights or affirmative action. Each day brings sad news about the reemergence of nooses and swastikas and the presence of hate groups and their hate crimes.

The one thing that our preaching should never lose is spontaneity and the ability either to focus upon or make some meaningful reference to events that may explode onto the national headlines or into a local community which could never have been anticipated when a schedule of preaching was being considered. Even if the preacher follows the lectionary, there needs to be a way to incorporate into sermons those unexpected events that deserve and even demand some attention. Do not be so wedded to any system of text and topic selection that you cannot either break away from it in order to focus on some significant current events or at the very least find a way to reference those events in the context of the sermon that had already been planned.

On the Sunday after September 11, 2001, every responsible preacher across America felt it important to break away from whatever their preplanned preaching schedule was, in order to preach a sermon that could put those catastrophic events in some biblical perspective—whether the preacher attempted to shape the sermon so as to assume a posture of pro-American sympathy for what appeared to be an unprovoked attack, or to view the events of that day within the context of the last quarter-century or so of U.S. foreign policy in the Middle East.

Many African American pastors faced this very challenge when racially charged issues emerged in the tiny town of Jena, Louisiana, between September of 2006 and September of 2007. On the Sunday either before or after the march on September 20, 2007, that brought sixty thousand people to that town of three thousand residents, a sermon on stewardship or the authority of Scripture would have been out of place in light of those events that demanded some word that spoke to the continuing challenge of race relations in the United States. Some preachers may have approached that day in complete sympathy with the so-called Jena 6. Others might have wondered how things might have been different if six black students had decided not to beat and stomp one white student, or how the first trial might have been different if the black people in Jena who were called for jury duty had shown up and been willing to serve. No matter which direction the sermon took, the challenge was to avoid simply preaching "about Jena" and to ask the question, What does our faith in Christ demand from us as a result of the events in that small town?[20]

Starting with Congregational Life

A similar starting point to the two just described involves issues, initiatives, and individual struggles going on within the life of the church itself at both the national and local levels. What does it mean to be Baptist or Lutheran or United Methodist at a time of rapid growth among nondenominational churches meeting in "worship centers" that do not display a cross and do not make reference to such biblical words as *sin* and *salvation*? What does it mean to be an Episcopalian at a time when the broader Anglican Church is reeling over the possibility of schism, driven by such issues as the ordination of openly gay clergy and an openly gay bishop? Sermons need to be shaped that help Christians think about their identity in Jesus Christ in a world that is increasingly secular on the one hand, and a world that is increasingly diverse in religious expression on the other hand. How do Christians navigate the waters between those who insist that America is "a Christian nation," and the fact that America is home to an increasing number of citizens who are adherents to Judaism, Islam, as well as to many other of the world's religions? The Bible can help shape sermons that can speak to those in this country who want to use the apparatus of organized religion in order to argue for certain public-policy positions on issues ranging from abortion to same-sex marriage to prayer in public schools.

Cleophus LaRue is helpful in thinking about the shift from church at denominational or national levels to the local level. Though his focus is primarily on preaching in the context of the black church, he offers some keen insights that have relevance for all cultural settings when it comes to sermons that speak to issues that involve what he calls the "maintenance of the institutional church."[21] His concerns range from sermons that focus on how to maintain the church's physical plant, to those practices that nurture spiritual formation, to insights on how church members should interact with one another. They include sermons on stewardship, missions and evangelistic activity, and faithfulness in church attendance. LaRue is correct when he observes that this kind of preaching "gives continued life and sustenance to the institutional church, which in turn reaffirms and upholds its participants."[22]

From Biblical Text to Sermonic Claim

Whether the question of "what to preach" starts with a biblical text, with a heart-wrenching question drawn from the drama of human life, some disturbing headline in the news, or an issue in church life, one thing remains the same—the sermon itself must be a message that is relevant to the lives and world of the listeners but which is rooted and centered in the exegesis of some biblical text. It is the informed use of Scripture as a source of authority in proclamation that distinguishes a sermon from the editorial page of a newspaper or a speech given by a policy maker. Either of those two could speak at length about such issues as nuclear war, world hunger, race relations, or the implications of columnist Thomas Friedman's observation that "the world is flat."[23] The editorial writer and the policymaker could base their statements on their personal opinions, on public-opinion polls, or on a particular political ideology that governs the newspaper's editorial page or the entity for which the policymaker is working. If that is all they did, no one would criticize them for how they went about their work.

That is not true for the preacher. It is not our personal opinion on any issue that is most important. It is not some well-informed update on the present status of any social or political issue that makes for an effective sermon. It should not be the liberal or conservative slant of the congregation, or of the preacher for that matter, that determines the content of the sermon on any given day. Rather, the sermon should be based upon the truths that are being taught and the lessons that can be learned from the biblical text that has been chosen or assigned for that day.

A sermon is that form of oral communication involving human beings in which our thoughts, beliefs, and what other noteworthy sources have said are all held up for scrutiny and analysis from the perspective of the Scriptures. Exegesis is the process by which the biblical text itself is held up for scrutiny so that we can more fully understand and appreciate its historical context, the meaning of its words and terms, the lessons that text intended to offer to its initial audience in antiquity, and the lessons it holds for us today.

This volume is not the place for a full-blown discussion about the importance of or the various methodologies for doing biblical exegesis.[24] Nevertheless, it would be impossible to talk about how to shape the claim of the sermon without talking to some degree about the role that exegesis plays right from the start in the way in which sermons are shaped. Exegesis has the potential to help the preacher discover the message of the biblical text in such a way as to understand better how that ancient message can be presented and grasped in some contemporary context. To be an effective preacher requires that those who design and deliver sermons should cultivate their skills in biblical exegesis.

For many years I have operated with an approach to biblical exegesis that involves eight steps, each one of which begins with the letter L.[25] The first five of these steps involve the background work that results in the best possible understanding of the biblical text which is being used as the focus of the sermon. The final three steps (especially the eighth one) will involve the actual preparation of the sermon itself. It is largely during that eighth step that preachers will be shaping the claim of their sermon. I will briefly review the process as a whole to set up the discussion of the move from exegesis to sermonic claim, from discovering what the text says to determining what the preacher will say.

The first step is called *Limits*, which is the initial determination about the amount of biblical material that will be used as the basis of any sermon. The second step is *Literature*, which seeks to discover what literary genre is being considered; history, laws, prophecy, wisdom materials, Gospels, epistles, poetry, apocalyptic, or biographical. There is no single way to preach all forms of biblical literature. Understanding the way a biblical genre works will help to shape the way the content of the sermon should be shaped. *Language* is the third step, which involves the search for the most accurate wording of the biblical text that is being studied. This step involves the use of Hebrew, Greek, and Aramaic when such facility is available. Where familiarity with the tools for original language study does not exist, this step involves studying the text in multiple, authoritative translations. Careful study of the language of the text will help us understand the intended claim the author is making.

Location is the fourth step and actually involves two separate considerations: the first involves studying the sociopolitical context in which the biblical passage is set (for instance, twelfth-century B.C.E. Egypt, Israel during the united kingdom, and first-century Judea under the rule of the Roman Empire). The second consideration involves the sociopolitical context in which the sermon on that text is going to be preached (for example, a working-class, black, inner-city congregation or an affluent, suburban megachurch). To determine an appropriate sermonic claim, we need to explore the connection of circumstances between these two locations. What element(s) of the human condition is found in both?

The fifth step in the process is called *Links*, which asks the question of whether there are other biblical texts that must be considered if the fullest understanding of the primary text is to be achieved. In many cases, the primary text upon which our sermons are based can be enhanced by looking at other relevant texts that shed light on the words used, the characters mentioned, the doctrines discussed, and/ or the locations in which those events are taking place. For example, many New Testament passages quote, refer to, or echo passages from the Old Testament.

The first five steps in this exegetical method reflect a standard approach to biblical exegesis that uses the insights and formulas of the so-called critical method. The next three steps in this methodology are less in line with the traditional, critical method for the study of biblical texts, and as such each of these next three steps will receive more detailed attention. They more explicitly begin the process of moving from the study toward the pulpit.

The sixth step is called *Leads*; it involves the decision about which of the characters in the text whose perspective will be that from which the text is read and preached. This could involve both major and minor characters, as well as people who are either virtuous and villainous. Paying attention to leads is especially important when the sermon is based upon a familiar passage of Scripture that might cause some listeners to assume that they already know where the sermon is headed. Preaching a familiar text from the perspective of a less-familiar character in that text can result in a fresh reading of the text and a more attentive audience as they are led down a path they have never before traveled. This step allows a single biblical text to become the basis of a sermon series as the text is considered and preached from the perspective of one character in the text after another.

The seventh step in this methodology is called *Lessons*. The objective here is to determine the message or messages that were intended for the original hearers and readers of the Bible, whether in the tenth century B.C.E. or the first century C.E. Nathan had a word for David when that king was at the height of his power. Jeremiah had a word for Zedekiah when the future of Judah was hanging in the balance. John the Baptist had a word for Herod Antipas that even kings are answerable to the sovereign God. Paul had a word for the Stoics and Epicureans in Athens who were gathered near the Acropolis in Athens, Greece, to debate and discuss the newest religious ideas. None of those words were offered with twenty-first-century North Americans in mind.

Before we can fully know what the Bible has to say to us in the twenty-first century we need to discern what the Bible was attempting to say to its various audiences in antiquity. What was the lesson Amos wanted Israel to learn about caring for the poor in the eighth century B.C.E.? What was the writer of Luke saying to people in the first century C.E. when he noted that Jesus was born in Bethlehem of Judea while Caesar Augustus and the Roman Empire controlled that region of the world?

Only after the text has been through these initial seven exegetical steps can we then move on to the eighth and final step, which is *Life Application,* or the actual development of the sermonic claim. There are two separate and distinct outcomes attached to this final step. First, this is when a concerted effort is made to shape a sermon that is relevant and compelling for a specific audience at a specific point in time. The objective of the preacher at this point is to declare what claim a particular biblical text is making upon a particular congregation or on a particular group of believers.

This eighth step also serves another wonderful purpose: namely, it becomes the point in the process of sermon design and delivery when the unique gifts and personality of each preacher are unlocked. What any preacher might see in a text or choose to say about that text in a sermon is substantially influenced by who they are and what life experiences and theological perspectives they bring to the preaching task. Each one of us is a combination of the wonderful gifts of heart, experience, culture, and mind that make us the persons that we are. Even if each one of us was to study the same biblical text and arrive at many of the same conclusions in terms of the first steps of the exegetical method mentioned earlier, when the time came for life application of that common text, the sermons that would be preached would undoubtedly be as diverse as the people for whom they are intended and the preacher who has prepared them. Each preacher has a unique "voice" with which she or he proclaims the word.

One way to understand this aspect of life application in preaching is to consider what Joseph Stowell says about preaching being done in two phases: the skill phase and the creative phase.[26] The *skill phase* is the technical work of doing biblical exegesis, which he equates with the task of shopping for the ingredients that will be used to bake a pie or a cake. The *creative phase* is the process of taking the results of the exegetical work and fashioning that material into a sermon. If the corollary for the skill phase is the person who shops for the ingredients for a cake or a pie, the corollary for the creative phrase is the cook or baker who skillfully mixes those items together and actually prepares a finished product that is straight from the oven. Two people can buy the same ingredients at the grocery store to bake the same dish. But the results can be quite different. Each baker mixes their ingredients in somewhat different ways; reflecting their personal tastes and their cultural preferences.

In preaching, as in baking, there is plenty of room for creativity and self-expression. Life application allows for the preacher to fashion sermonic content that works best with the gifts he or she has in the context where he or she is called upon to preach. Careful and systematic exegesis of the biblical text should always precede any attempt to write a sermonic claim. Exegesis allows the text to speak for itself, and it prevents the preacher from twisting the text to serve his or her agenda for the day. Only through careful research into the text has the preacher gained enough understanding of what is at stake in the text that he or she is ready to determine what word he or she will offer to the congregation. Once study of the text is concluded, preachers must shape a singular, sermonic claim that began with the word of Scripture but is appropriate to their particular pastoral, homiletical voice and is relevant for their particular audience.

One way to be sure that the exegetical process has been thoroughly explored, and also to be sure that all of the homiletical options for a given passage have been considered, is to begin to shape a sermon whose central claim can be stated in a single sentence with no semi-colons or parenthetical clauses. If the claim of the sermon cannot be stated in one clear and succinct sentence, then the preacher is probably still thinking about what it is that he or she wants to say in the life application stage of the exegetical process.

This one-sentence approach to sermon design can be extremely helpful to a preacher as it forces the sermon to move away from all of the valuable information that may have been uncovered in the exegetical process, and challenges the preacher finally to arrive at the point where the sermon can be about one clear and specific theme or topic that can be stated and restated throughout the sermon. It can become the title or the opening sentence of the sermon. However the preacher uses the one-sentence statement in the actual design of the sermon, the designing of the sermon should not begin unless and until that one-sentence statement has been determined.

The idea of developing a one-sentence statement that sharpens the claim of the sermon is in keeping with what terms and concepts referenced earlier in this chapter. Remember the "big idea" of Haddon Robinson, the "focus statement" of Thomas Long, the "theme statement" of Fred Craddock, or the "the proposition" of Samuel Proctor."[27] Each of these approaches is a way to go about shaping that single sentence around which the central claim of the sermon will be determined. As was stated earlier in the shift from lessons to life application, this is the step where the voice and perspective of each preacher will most clearly be heard.

Ten preachers might all agree to preach on the same text, whether it is assigned by the lectionary, arrived at by *lectio continua,* or adopted by common consent. Their exegetical findings in terms of language issues, literary genre, sociopolitical setting, and even the meaning of that text to its original, ancient audience might end up in perfect agreement. However, it is in the shift from exegesis (what the text says) to sermon design (what is the message of that text going to be to a specific contemporary audience), that the unique voice of each of those ten preachers is most likely to be heard. Each of them is likely to come up with their own one-sentence statement concerning the central claim they want to make in that sermon, from that text, to their particular audience.

I refer back to the definition of a sermonic claim stated earlier in this book. "Every sermon needs to make *one* clear, compelling, biblically centered, and contextually relevant claim that sets some aspect of God's will and God's word before some specific segment of God's people. This is done with the hope that those people will be challenged, informed, corrected, or encouraged as a result of the word set before them that day."[28]

The Postmodern Challenge

Given the rise of what is labeled postmodernity, some may question the wisdom of the preacher focusing a sermon on "*one* clear, compelling, biblically centered, and contextually relevant claim that sets some aspect of God's will and God's word before some specific segment of God's people." There are some people who challenge the authority of Scripture in the twenty-first century. There are some who advocate for or practice a generalized, individualized spirituality instead of a biblically oriented, communal faith. Others argue that one path to God is as good as any other, so why should a person pay any more attention to what the Bible says than they do to what any other book or any other religious tradition has to say? In some church circles various forms of communication such as PowerPoint presentations, video clips, and small-group discussions take the place of the sermon. Sanctuaries are being referred to as auditoriums that are designed not to include a cross or any other noticeable Christian symbols. The "pulpit" is being replaced by a "podium." Worship services are being replaced with classes, spiritual formation events, and motivational messages.

It cannot be doubted that we are living in an age when the preacher can no longer assume belief in the authority of Scripture, much less familiarity with its content, in the congregation. We can also agree that we are living at a time when other religious traditions and approaches to spirituality are heard and seen everywhere we turn. That being said, those factors should not result in our sounding either retreat or surrender so far as our commitment to biblical preaching is concerned. Several helpful books have been written that assist preachers with going about their work in this postmodern context.[29]

As preachers we should be conscious of the postmodern challenges that confront us if we want our sermons to be culturally relevant. This does not mean, however, that we should be intimidated or afraid to set forth Word-based sermonic claims. Some historical perspective is helpful. This is not the first time in history the biblical message has had to struggle in order to be heard. But that word has never gone silent.

The postmodern world in which we preach is no more difficult a context for preaching than was the eighth-century B.C.E. world of Amos, the
seventh-century B.C.E. world of Jeremiah, or the first-century C.E. world
of Christ or Paul. All of them preached a biblical message in a world
that either was unfamiliar with their scriptural authorities, unwilling to
conform to them, or committed to other religious practices altogether.
Our preaching predecessors were not put off by those realities. They
simply preached "in season and out of season" (2 Tim. 4:2, NIV).

Sometimes their words were heeded. Sometimes their words
were heard and considered. Sometimes their words were completely
ignored. There is little doubt that Jeremiah faced a far more hostile
and unwelcoming climate for his preaching than is the case for any
of us today. His preaching about idolatry and corruption in the nation
fell on deaf ears, but he continued to preach. His scrolls were cut up
and contemptuously tossed into the fire by King Jehoiakim (Jer. 36:23-
24), he was thrown into a cistern filled with mud as punishment for
his unwelcome words (Jer. 38:1-10). Nevertheless, the prophet spoke
words that give full expression to what every preacher in the postmodern world must feel from time to time:

> O LORD, you have enticed me,
>   and I was enticed;
> you have overpowered me,
>   and you have prevailed;
> I have become a laughingstock all day long;
>   everyone mocks me.
> For whenever I speak, I must cry out.
>   I must shout "Violence and destruction!"
> For the word of the LORD has become for me
>   a reproach and derision all day long. (Jer. 20:7-8)

The words of Jeremiah could have been written with the preaching
climate of the twenty-first century in mind. Preaching is lightly
regarded and the gospel is rarely heeded in a culture that prefers the
opinions of scientists, pop-music icons, and public policymakers over
anything that comes wrapped in the phrase, "Thus says the LORD."

That being said, we should not only identify with the challenges
faced by Jeremiah in preaching the word of God in an unfriendly and

unwelcoming world, but we should seek to match his determination to continue to preach a faithful, biblically centered message no matter how hostile or dismissive the environment may be for what we have to say. That is how Jeremiah continued to describe his preaching context:

> If I say, "I will not mention him
> or speak any more in his name,"
> Then within me there is something like a burning fire
> shut up in my bones.
> I am weary of holding it in;
> and I cannot. (Jer. 20:9).

Paul experienced a similar problem of being heard by some but dismissed or denounced by others in his sermon in Athens in Acts 17:32-34. Surely Paul's attempt to preach about Christ, and especially about the resurrection of Christ in the presence of Stoics and Epicureans (Acts 17:17-18) corresponds to our challenge of preaching Christ in this postmodern world. Paul, challenging the superficial religiosity and the false gods he encountered at the Areopagus (Acts 17:22-31), reflects our challenge of preaching about Christ in a culture that is content with private spirituality that views any path to God as being just as true and valid as any other. We can easily recognize the various responses to Paul's preaching—the same has happened to us. What is of greater importance and of far-greater urgency is for all of us to be willing to identify with Paul's determination to preach Christ in a culture that is unfriendly, disinterested, or largely unfamiliar with our vocabulary and our values. There is no more uncompromising declaration of the gospel message than is found in Paul's sermon in Athens when he says: "Because he has fixed a day on which he will have the world judged in righteousness by a man whom he has appointed, and of this he has given assurance to all by raising him from the dead" (Acts 17:31).

That is what we should be preaching and that is the claim that our sermons should be setting forth—what God wants to say to the church and to the world, as that message is found in the Scriptures. Our task as preachers is to delve into that message, select out some portion of it that will be the basis for a particular sermon, and then

preach that message in a way that is biblically centered and culturally relevant. Our task is to be an instrument through which a word
of ultimate significance claims our congregations in a transformative
manner. And it is our task to do this week after week, every time we
step into the pulpit.

Chapter 2

So What?

*. . . we cannot help speaking about what
we have seen and heard. —Acts 4:20*

In chapter 1, I argued that the people in the pew should be rewarded with a sermon that is worth paying attention to—a significant word should be offered to them. One way of reminding ourselves of this demand on the preacher is to think about how much time a congregation has invested in the process of assembling itself together on any given Sunday morning. When preachers think about the time invested in preparing for the sermon, we often make the mistake of only calculating the time we take in the preparation of the sermon. We can be intimidated by the oft-quoted axiom of Harry Emerson Fosdick that preachers should spend one hour in preparation for every one minute of sermon delivery. For him that usually equated to twenty hours of weekly preparation, since his sermons were usually about twenty minutes long.

This pulpit-centered approach to preaching has many drawbacks, not the least of which is the unspoken assumption that the only person whose time really matters is the preacher. The truth is, there is a vastly larger amount of time being invested in the sermon by the one hundred, or five hundred, or even one thousand or more persons who get up, get dressed, get out the front door of their residence, get through some distance to the church building, and finally get settled in to be a part of the worship service. Let us assume that an average American worship service consists of one hundred attendees. Let us also assume that each of those one hundred persons spends two hours getting ready for and traveling to church. Let us also assume that the worship service they attend will last for one hour. The preacher may have spent twenty hours of preparation to deliver a twenty-minute sermon, but the congregation as a whole will have spent three hundred hours in order to be in place to hear the sermon that day. That much time dare not be wasted by preachers who have nothing of substance or urgency to say.

There is an anonymous poem that has challenged me as I think about making the best use of my own time and the time entrusted to me by the congregations I have served or preached to over the last thirty-five years. This poem is frequently spoken within the African American church context, probably because so many graduates of Morehouse College who are now in the ministry remember hearing these words from Benjamin Mays when he preached in the college chapel.

> I have only just a minute,
> only 60 seconds in it,
> forced upon me, didn't choose it,
> didn't seek it, can't refuse it,
> so it's up to me to use it,
> have to suffer if I lose it,
> pay a price if I abuse it,
> just a tiny little minute,
> but eternity is in it.

That is what is at stake when we preach. What we say in our few minutes has consequences, for better or for worse, and can yield dividends for life or for death, for all of eternity. We need to hold ourselves accountable for the use of the "tiny little minute" entrusted to us. We should take great care not to abuse the investment of precious minutes offered up to us week after week by the people who gather to worship God and who will, in that context, hear our sermons.

It is bad enough when preachers waste their own time splashing around in the shallow water of positive thinking, prosperity theology, or narrowly defined "moral values" like arguments against homosexuality or abortion while leaving completely unaddressed such justice issues as war and peace in Iraq, global climate change, the forty-five million Americans who have no health insurance, and the conditions facing the two million Americans confined in prison—not to mention the 80 percent of those prisoners who would be better served by drug treatment that costs five thousand dollars annually than by incarceration that costs seven times that amount each year. That does not include the stunning divorce rate that threatens one out of every two heterosexual marriages, the anxiety and hysteria associated with terrorism, the outsourcing of jobs from America, the steadily rising cost of living that is pushing more and more families into poverty, and the continuing presence of racism and bigotry that is increasingly taking the form of nooses being hung and swastikas being painted in public places. Time is too precious to be wasted on pointless preaching. There are serious problems and agonizing concerns that confront people at the deepest emotional and existential levels every day. When they make the effort and invest the time to come out to worship on Sunday morning, many of them are coming with the words of Jeremiah 37:17 burning in their hearts; "Is there any word from the Lord?" When the sermon is over, those in the pew should have been moved in such a way that they can answer in the affirmative, "Yes, today there was a word from the Lord for me."

Don't Waste a Minute
Because the time commitment of the congregation is so great, we should not waste a single minute of the time of the sermon. People in today's world will not listen very long to anyone or anything that does not make a strong and compelling appeal for their attention.

Communication Overload
One of the reasons for such audience impatience is that we live in a world where many people watch TV with a program guide in one hand and a remote control in the other. At any point in any program those viewers are ready to shift the channel away from anything that does not interest, amuse, or challenge them. Viewers usually give a TV program a very small amount of time to win them over into watching the remainder of the broadcast. That time can range from thirty seconds to two minutes within which something needs to be said or shown that is sufficiently

interesting to those viewers to keep them tuned to that station. If it does not happen within that limited period of time, you can be sure the finger that is already on the remote control channel button will soon be hard at work surfing for something else to view. People will not endure for very long anything that is not interesting; they will change the channel.

This dynamic is multiplied when we consider the complete overload of communication we receive these days. Not only do people get loads of unsolicited junk mail, they receive e-mail, instant messages, text messages, faxes, phone calls and voice mail on multiple phones (home, office, and cellular), newsletters, billboard and bulletin board announcements, and interoffice memos that float back and forth all day. Many people may be on information overload. There is so much information and communication coming at them all the time, their only defense is to screen out what they will and will not consider.

Here is a news flash for us preachers: the people who are bombarded with messages all week and watch TV with their finger always at the ready on the remote control are the same people who gather together on Sunday mornings. We need to understand that they will listen to our sermons with the same basic disposition they have toward all these other forms of communication. They will not listen long to a sermon that seems to have no obvious and immediate bearing on their emotional engagement in the ebb and flow of life.

We who are preaching the gospel must learn how to communicate in such a way that we can gain a hearing in the midst of all the messages and mailings that are clamoring for people's attention. This may mean that preachers need to become more proficient with technology themselves. Video projection systems and PowerPoint presentations as part of the sermon (displaying the Scripture text, highlighting some crucial point, playing a relevant video clip, or just giving people a close-up view of the preacher) can help twenty-first-century audiences feel more closely drawn to the pulpit and the preacher. Technology alone is not the answer, however. Plainly stated, preachers need to develop the ability to make listeners feel emotionally claimed by the content of the sermon.

The Age of Televangelism

Another reason congregations are impatient with sermons is that the same mass communication technology described above brings with it yet another challenge for those who will be preaching on a regular basis before live audiences in small to midsized congregations. Parish preachers are going to be up against the polish and pizazz of high-powered cable TV evangelists who broadcast their slick sermons right into the homes of the very people the local pastor is trying to reach. These people are not simply evangelists who happen to employ the media of radio and television. They are marketing and communications experts with studio production crews that rival network television programs. These TV ministries have honed the skill of capturing and holding a TV audience. They invite (and too often manipulate) the television viewer to become emotionally involved not only through the words the preacher is saying but also through choreographed staging, professional music, constantly changing camera angles, and pictures of the most enthusiastic members of the "studio" audience. These media messengers are most often out to get donations or sell some product in addition to their presentation of the gospel—the minister's most recent books, CDs, prayers for physical healing, or secrets to achieving financial prosperity. It is because they are as much marketers as they are evangelists that they have perfected the hooks commonly used in all areas of sales that get someone's attention and then drives them to buy whatever is being offered.

As a result, for better or worse, when pastors of local churches stand up to speak, they are not only competing with the multitude of messages that come at people every day from secular society in general, they are also competing with the Christian media messengers who are increasingly defining what hearers expect out of preaching.

Connect with the Audience as Quickly as Possible

Preachers, therefore, cannot afford to waste a minute in catching and holding the congregation's attention. We need to be aware of the fact that from the moment we open our mouths in the pulpit, people in the pews are consciously and unconsciously asking themselves, "So what?" or "What does this have to do with me?" This is not an idle question. It is a question of great urgency to both the preacher and the listener. For the listeners a sense that the sermon does indeed have something to do with their lives must come early in the sermon, or else their minds will begin to tune out the preacher and they will start thinking about other things. In his classic communications book,

Public Speaking as Listeners Like It, Richard Borden names this dynamic "Ho Hum."[1] He describes Ho Hum in this way: "Do not picture your audience as waiting with eager eyes and bated breath to catch your message. Picture it, instead, as definitely bored—and distinctly suspicious that you are going to make this situation worse."[2]

What this means for preachers is that we must be aware that from the moment we stand up and begin to preach, the clock is ticking as to how long people will continue to pay close attention to what is being said. We must get the hearers emotionally engaged at the beginning of the sermon if we want them to stay with us until the end of the sermon.

To use an athletic analogy, preachers should think of their work more like that of a sprinter in the one-hundred-meter dash than of a long-distance runner in the twenty-six-mile marathon. When the starting gun sounds for a marathon run, it is not required that the runners get off to an explosive start—they have miles to run and hours ahead of them before they approach the finish line. They can pace themselves and save most of their energy for the final miles of the race. Not so in the one-hundred-meter dash. In order to have any chance at all, the sprinter must explode out of the starting blocks and hit full stride within seconds. Success for a sprinter requires getting off to a good start. The same is true for preachers: success requires getting off to a good start. That means that the most important sentence in the sermon is the first sentence. The most important paragraph in the sermon is the first paragraph. The most important time frame is the first three to five minutes. Every effort must be made at the beginning of the sermon to make the case for why people should pay attention to what is going to follow. As Borden puts it, "Your speech is not well organized unless you kindle a quick flame of spontaneous interest *in your first* sentence."[3] This is not simply an intellectual endeavor. It requires the use of a searching question, a compelling comment or observation, a riveting illustration, or an appeal to some current event that the preacher wants to review from a faith perspective. Early in the sermon people need to know what is coming, and they need to know that it is interesting or relevant or essential for their development as Christians.

This argument may appear to put me in conflict with the approach to preaching in my own African American context commonly referred to as "Start low—go slow—catch fire and retire." In point of fact, there is no conflict. This adage about "start low—go slow" actually has much more to do with the passion and zeal that is so often associated with delivery in black preaching. This phrase is a warning for those preachers who tend to start out their sermons "in high gear" both in terms of pace and volume. When you reach that level of energy and enthusiasm at the beginning of the sermon, you leave yourself with nowhere to go as the sermon heads toward its conclusion.

The advice that is being offered here is not to start out with maximum enthusiasm and give away the sermonic claim at the beginning. Rather, it is to raise the "so what" question as quickly as possible. Point out to people what is coming and why it is important for them to listen. You do not have ten minutes in order to make a connection with the listeners. You have two to three minutes to get their attention. There will be plenty of time to "catch fire" and "retire" once a solid connection has been made with the audience over what is being preached and why that message is important to those listeners. The hearers need to be emotionally involved early on; they need to be claimed by the sermon from the beginning.

Claiming the congregation's emotional and existential engagement at the beginning of the sermon does not mean giving away all we plan to say from the get-go. To sustain interest throughout the sermon, some things must be held back, some tension must be left that needs resolving, some questions raised that need answering. Preachers might want to consider a methodology described by Eugene Lowry. He talks about establishing a clear and quick connection with the congregation through the intersection of the "problematic itch," which is something of interest or curiosity for the audience, and the "solutional scratch," which is the answer or the way forward being offered by the sermon.[4]

Lowry encourages the preacher to begin the sermon with something that is, or can be made to be, of interest to the congregation, and then use the balance of the sermon to shed light on or to bring some resolution to that issue. This approach to preaching would work regardless of the sermon style or format that is being used. You could move from the "problematic itch" to the "solutional scratch" when the preacher is delivering a textual or expository sermon where the problematic involves a hard-to-understand passage that can now be explained. It works if the preacher is delivering a topical sermon on a controversial issue or an urgent, current event that can be considered from a biblical and theological perspective. Whether the format is biblical storytelling, a doctrinal discussion, or even a biographical (first-person) sermon, Lowry offers a reliable way to establish an early, solid, emotionally engaged connection with the listeners.

Perhaps it is helpful to offer an example of connecting with the congregation quickly. In a recent sermon at Antioch Baptist Church in Cleveland, I preached on the subject "Take Time To Be Holy," based on 1 Peter 1:13-16. The sermon began with a brief introduction to A. J. Jacobs's book, *The Year of Living Biblically*.[5] The book had been in the news for many weeks prior to that Sunday, and many people had heard Jacobs being interviewed on various TV channels. There was already a certain amount of "buzz" about this book, and I wanted to capitalize on that existing interest in order to make a biblical and theological point.

I reflected on how Jacobs set out for one year to adapt his life to the religious laws of the Old Testament; giving special attention to not cutting his hair or shaving off his beard. I then noted that at the end of that one-year period Jacobs cut off his nearly foot-long beard and hair and returned to his former appearance and his former way of living. I then suggested to the listeners that many of us do much the same thing; we come to church periodically, go through the weekly rituals of worship, but revert back to our former selves as soon as the service is dismissed. God does not want us to live biblically for a year or for two hours on Sunday. God wants us to live biblically *period*. So within minutes, hearers were invited to examine their own lives and ask whether they lived schizophrenically—a dual life of secular and biblical existence. After this, I shifted to the text in 1 Peter and unpacked what it means to accept the call to be holy as God is holy.

Pathos

In the previous chapter, I referred to Aristotle's three principles of rhetoric or public speaking: *logos*, *pathos*, and *ethos*. Chapter 1 was primarily related to *logos*, the content of the sermon. We shift now from that consideration of beginning with the word to a consideration of Aristotle's second principle of rhetoric, *pathos*. Whereas *logos* refers to *intellectual* appeal, *pathos* is the *emotional* appeal of the speech.

Anything worth saying is worth saying with passion and enthusiasm and conviction. The emotions of the speaker stir the emotions of the audience.

Emotion, Not Emotionalism

Before arguing what type of emotion should be sought in the sermon event, it is important to name what is *not* appropriate. There is a difference between *inviting* the congregation into an emotional and existential engagement of the gospel and *manipulating* the emotions of the congregation. It is the difference between involving the congregation emotionally and the preacher giving in to the temptation of emotionalism. Emotion for its own sake is emotionalism. Too many preachers preach as if simply getting louder and louder and more and more emotional is the primary goal and measurement of effective preaching. The rush to emotionalism, sometimes to the exclusion of content, is called "getting to the gravy." The idea is that certain foods should not be served unless they are covered with gravy. Hence, not to have any gravy, in eating or in preaching, results in an incomplete and unsatisfying experience.

But the assumption behind such emotionalism is that volume and enthusiasm can take the place of substance and relevant content. Charles Chauncy attacked such emotionalism (which he called "Enthusiasm") in a sermon in Boston in 1742. He stated:

> I am in the first place, to give you some account of Enthusiasm. The word from its etymology carries in it a good meaning, as signifying inspiration from God; in which sense the prophets under the Old Testament and the apostles under the new might properly be called Enthusiasts. But the word is more commonly used in a bad sense, as intending an imaginary, not a real inspiration. An Enthusiast mistakes the workings of his own passions for divine communications, and fancies himself immediately inspired by the Spirit of God, when all the while he is under no other influence than that of an over-heated imagination.[6]

We can counterbalance the tendency toward emotionalism highlighted in "getting to the gravy" with another adage from the African American preaching tradition: "Good meat makes its own gravy."[7] This adage suggests that if the preacher has something substantive to say, and if the preacher develops that sermon idea in ways which demonstrate its relevance and importance to the listeners, the listener's emotional involvement will occur naturally. While many foods are better when covered in gravy, gravy isn't very satisfying unless it has something to cover.

Emotion in the Pulpit

Having warned against emotionalism as a way toward manipulating a response from the listeners, let me argue for the importance of *authentic* emotions in the sermon event. The issue of *pathos* moves the discussion about preaching from the question of "what to preach" to the question, "So what?" Enthusiasm and deep-seated conviction signal to the listeners that what is being said by the preacher is of the utmost importance and deserves their attention. If the subject matter being preached about does not generate any passion or enthusiasm from the preacher who is delivering the sermon it is not very likely that the sermon will generate much interest, much less emotional engagement, among those to whom the sermon is directed. In the beginning there must be a word, but that word must be preached with boldness and conviction or else the audience will lose interest very quickly. W. Floyd Breese puts it well in an essay entitled "Emotion in Preaching,"

> You may use logic to convince a person of your point of view. But emotion is required before that person will act upon that conviction. Preaching that merely tells people what they ought to do is futile. Most already know what they ought to do. How do you move a listener's thinking from "ought to" to "want to"? Add emotion. People mainly do those things they feel like doing.[8]

Preaching is not just the task and skill of developing something to say. It is also the art and the determination to relay that message with a sense of urgency and authority which inspires a congregation to embrace fully what is said. On more than one occasion I have heard Gardner C. Taylor, the majestic preacher from Brooklyn, speak about preaching as both a "matter" and a "manner." The "matter" involves what you have come to say in your sermon. The "manner" involves the way in which that matter is delivered. It involves passion, enthusiasm, conviction, zeal, earnestness, urgency, or any other synonym which suggests that what is being said deserves to be heard because it is of the utmost importance.

As we go about the task of preaching in the twenty-first century, there is much that can be learned by taking note of the urgency and conviction that was the hallmark of the preaching of Peter and John in Jerusalem as recorded in Acts 4. Their preaching was so compelling that people gave them a hearing whether they agreed with what they were saying or not. Not only did they have something to say (*what*), but they said it in ways that made it clear that it was important for people to pay attention to their message (*so what*).

Acts 4 begins with Peter and John being imprisoned by the leaders of the Temple in Jerusalem because they were creating a disturbance by preaching about Christ and about the resurrection of the dead. Despite the fact that their message was rejected by the religious leaders in Jerusalem, many who heard them preaching came to believe in Christ. Within a matter of days, the message about Jesus Christ had attracted over five thousand followers. After one night in jail, Peter and John are brought before the religious authorities to be questioned about what they were preaching.

Peter serves as the spokesperson for the pair. This is the same Peter who, on the night before the crucifixion of Jesus, had denied three times that he even knew Christ. Now he is standing before the very men who had sought to have Christ condemned to death and whom he feared might condemn him on that fateful night if his connection to Jesus had been confirmed. This time, however, he does not deny knowing Christ. This time he is not seeking to avoid any direct connection between himself and Jesus. This time he is declaring the power of Jesus Christ that had allowed John and him to heal a crippled man, and he speaks this way inside the meeting hall of the Sanhedrin.

Having heard his words and having been duly impressed with his boldness, the Sanhedrin confers for a time and then decides to order Peter and John to cease from any further preaching in the name of Jesus or about the words and deeds of Jesus. Their exact words are, "Speak no more to anyone in this name" (Acts 4:17). With their bodies still aching from one night in an uncomfortable jail cell, and with the possibility of many more days in jail, or worse, looming before them, Peter speaks words that reflect both his confidence and his conviction; "We cannot help speaking about what we have heard and seen."

That is an example of what contributed to the effectiveness of apostolic preaching. It was based in a deep conviction that they had something to say and they must say it! That is why the early church was able to win thousands of converts to a new message. That is what won them a hearing in every town and village, and in every synagogue and on every street corner where they stopped to preach. They had a manner that matched their matter. They had something important to say, and they said it with courage and conviction that could not be silenced or intimidated. They had something important to say, and they were going to say it no matter what! And this touched both the minds and hearts of their audiences. The apostles were a powerful fusion of *logos* and *pathos*! As I have argued elsewhere, enthusiastic preaching was indeed part of the overarching biblical tradition:

> Somehow I do not envision any of the prophets, or Paul, or Jesus being first and foremost concerned about whether they were being perceived as being too emotional. They spoke with urgency, with conviction, and with a sense of purpose that was so compelling that they evoked an almost immediate response from those who heard them.
>
> Sometimes the response was conversion and faith in Christ. Sometimes the response was rejection and the need to flee the city to preserve their lives (Acts 19). But either way, it is easy to imagine that it was their obvious sense of conviction, of emotion, of passion (pathos) that moved the crowds who heard them. I sincerely doubt whether cold and dispassionate preaching would have resulted in "turning the world upside down" (Acts 17:6).[9]

Of course, we need not go all the way back to biblical times to find emotional expression being an essential element of proclamation. Passion in preaching is rooted in the history of American preaching. In many African American churches, such words as celebration, intonation, musicality, whooping, and rhythm have served to describe not only the manner in which the sermonic conclusion is presented but also the way in which the preacher is emotionally invested throughout the sermon.[10]

Henry H. Mitchell notes that the use of passion or emotion in preaching may be the greatest point of divergence between black and white preaching in America today. He demonstrates, however, that this was not always the case. In his article, "African American Preaching: The Future of a Rich Tradition," Mitchell notes that "The first Great Awakening burst forth with shouting . . . under no less worthy of a preacher than Jonathan Edwards. . . . The shouting really burst forth under Whitefield and the Tennents. . . . An ex-slave named Gustavus Vassa, in his autobiographical slave narrative tells how greatly he was impressed by the 'fervor and earnestness' of George Whitefield."[11] The likes of Whitefield, Edwards, Gilbert Tennent, and John Wesley were among the targets of Chauncy's attack on Enthusiasm mentioned above, so we must be careful that our counterbalance to emotionalism not be an *over*-corrective. We must not pull so strongly against emotionalism that we leave the sermon devoid of emotion. There are far too many preachers today who, for fear of being viewed as having an "over-heated imagination," deliver their sermons without any energy or passion. Part of what made preaching so effective during the Great Awakening was that it was forceful and compelling. Part of what makes much preaching today so ineffective is that it is dull and is delivered without "fervor and earnestness."

Halford Luccock, who taught homiletics at Yale Divinity School for many years, made an observation about himself that might apply to many other preachers as well. In his book *Communicating the Gospel*, Luccock said: "Eugene Ormandy once dislocated his shoulder while leading the Philadelphia Orchestra. I do not know what they were playing, but he was giving all of himself to it. And I have asked myself sadly, did I ever dislocate anything while preaching, even a necktie?"[12]

Like our forebears, we who are preaching in cities and towns across America and around the world in the twenty-first century also have something important to say, and we must approach our work with the urgency that suggests that we are going to say it no matter what. The gospel of Jesus Christ has something significant and distinct to say to a world that is so deeply diseased with poverty, violence, drug addiction, domestic violence, racial and gender discrimination, global warming, war, terrorism, fear, and loneliness that no amount of consumer goods can remedy. The time has surely come to lift up our message with as much authentic enthusiasm and conviction as did our biblical forebears if we hope to make an impact on our hearers at the level of deep emotional transformation.

Emotion in Worship

While this book is about shaping the claim of the sermon, it is important for preachers to remember that their sermons and the people
who hear them are themselves shaped by the wider liturgical context
in which their preaching occurs. The time that people invest is not
entirely committed to the sermon. While the sermon does not lose its
importance, or its centrality in many church settings, it is important for
us to keep in mind that God can "show up" and "show out" in more
that one spot in the worship service.

The fact is, people can be blessed and their souls can be strengthened—they can be emotionally stirred and existentially moved—by cho-
ral and congregational music, by corporate prayer, and by the reading of
Scripture, creeds, or litanies. Remembering that many Protestant bodies
refer to a ministry of Word and Sacrament, there is great inspiration and
insight that occurs during the moments when the congregation shares in
the ordinances or sacraments of baptism and communion. In fact, every
preacher should thank God that the congregation is not totally depen-
dent upon the preacher to deliver the people into the presence of God.
If that were the case, and our sermons happened not to connect with
the congregation on any given day, there could be many people who
attended that worship service returning home unfed and unfulfilled.

Thankfully, on many a Sunday when the words of the preacher do
not connect with the hearts and minds of everyone who is seated in
the congregation, the Holy Spirit touches the congregation through
the uplifting anthem by the choir, the heartfelt prayer lifted up by a
deacon, the passing of the peace, the personal testimony of someone
else in attendance, or the sharing of bread and wine. Even when we
preach one of our best sermons, we must remember that what we
do and say as preachers is still part of a wider worship experience
where the input and involvement of others is as important as anything
we might say or do. It is the whole of the worship service—prayers,
praise, and proclamation—that invites those in the pew to experience,
emotionally and existentially, a level of involvement in the good news
that is comforting or confronting, that is transformative.

Emotion in the Pews

I mentioned earlier that John Wesley preached with great emotional
fervor and passion. However, John Wesley is not only a good point of

reference for emotion in the pulpit; he is an equally valid point of reference for sermons that can stir up emotions in the pews as well. Wesley had spent years under the uninspired instruction of eighteenth-century Anglican priests, and that proved not to be enough to sustain him during his initial evangelistic efforts both in England and among the native people of Georgia in colonial America between 1736 and 1738. By the time Wesley returned to England in 1738, he was discouraged and uncertain about his faith and about his vocation in ministry.

Having established a relationship with the Moravians while he had been in America, he found himself attending a worship service at a small Moravian church on Aldersgate Street in London on May 24, 1738. As that service proceeded, Wesley reported, "I felt my heart strangely warmed." Not only did Wesley *hear* something, as was undoubtedly the case in his earlier experiences in the Anglican church, but this time he also *felt* something, which apparently had not been the case in his earlier experience. The emotion present in the Moravian preacher was not limited to the pulpit. It reached out and touched the heart of John Wesley.

This ought to be the goal for our preaching today, 270 years after Wesley's Aldersgate experience. There needs to be enough passion and emotion in the heart of the preacher that our sermons are able to "warm the hearts" of those who are seated in the pews. We are not preaching simply to inform or instruct. That was precisely what Wesley found to be so unfulfilling about the sermons he had heard earlier in his life. Our sermons should be preached in such a way that we have the chance to "move" people in two distinct ways. First, we should seek to move them at the level of their emotions. We should seek to stir them, encourage them, and inspire them as they come to grips with the issues that confront them from day to day. That being accomplished, we should seek to move them in a second way, that is, by attempting to move them into some appropriate response to what they have heard us say.

However, it is unlikely that we will be able to move people into action after the sermon is over and after the service is complete if we are not first able to move them, to stir them, or to "warm their hearts" while they are seated in the pews. Thinking again of John Wesley, it is likely that nothing he was able to accomplish whether during the First Great Awakening or when he laid down the foundations for the

Methodist movement would have taken place had he not first been emotionally touched that night at Aldersgate. Thus, in discussing the role of emotion or pathos in preaching, it is as important that we create some emotion in the pews as it is that we display emotion ourselves while we are preaching.

The same warning that was raised earlier about manipulated and manipulative emotionalism that is so often on display by those who occupy the pulpit in our churches, applies equally well to those who occupy the pews from Sunday to Sunday. The goal of preaching is not simply to generate an emotional response as an end in itself, and the response to effective preaching does not need to be an eruption of emotionalism, as some preachers and listeners seem to believe. The goal of preaching is to present the claims of the gospel in general, and the claim of any sermon in particular, in ways that appeal both to the head and to the heart. The goal of preaching is to speak the truths of Scripture in a way that relates to and connects with the lives of people so that they will feel there has been a word from the Lord for them on that day. That can more likely happen when the sermon is able to tap into the legitimate range of emotions that stand at the heart of the gospel message.

Preaching has the capacity to stir up a wide range of legitimate emotions within the listeners without attempting to draw people into manipulated and sometimes orchestrated acts of emotionalism. Sermons should be able to stir up the emotion of joy so that people can literally rejoice in the goodness of God and in the joy of their own salvation. The gospel is about "good news," and the best response to good news is joy. There are times when the desired emotion takes the shape of assurance or reassurance as people are reminded that God can sustain and deliver them no matter how difficult things might become at any given point in their lives. Given the ever-present nature of sickness, death, tragedy, hardship, and loss, it is appropriate for our sermons occasionally to tap into the emotion of consolation that causes people to feel strengthened and soothed in the face of the great pains they may recently have endured.

Contrition and repentance are emotions that preaching should be able to generate. I am not suggesting that preachers intentionally send people on a guilt trip, but we should make people aware of the reality of sin both within them as well as within the preacher, and then we should point out to them the availability of God's grace, mercy, love, and forgiveness. When these themes are preached with passion and conviction they will generate a legitimate emotional response in the pews. The Bible is full of instances when the preaching of Jesus generated this very kind of emotional response from the people of first-century Palestine. When done with integrity the same deep emotional connection can be made with people in the twenty-first century as well.

Hope is another valid emotion that can be generated by our preaching. Life does not have to remain the same forever for those who are facing oppression or suffering in this life. The God who delivered Israel from slavery in Egypt and Daniel from the lions' den can also deliver us from the dangers and perils that we confront today, whether those dangers and perils are economic, political, or physical. Hope can be extended beyond matters of this life and this world, because the same power that raised Jesus from the dead is able to deliver us not only from the futility of life but also from the finality of death. First Corinthians 15:20-22 is a word of hope that can resonate with every person in the pews: "But in fact Christ has been raised from the dead, the first fruits of those who have died . . . for as all die in Adam, so all will be made alive in Christ."

Pathos is not limited to the passion of the person who delivers the sermon; it must have its corollary in the pew where people are able to be moved and stirred by what they have heard. Before people can be expected to respond to the message of the sermon and take some particular action, they must hear a message that involves the emotions of the preacher and is able to tap into the emotions of those seated in the pews. Once the hearts of people have been "strangely warmed" it is more likely that they will act upon the words they have heard. By contrast, any sermon, no matter how much emotion is displayed by the preacher, may not be fully effective if that sermon does not make a legitimate emotional connection with the people in the pews.

Make It Plain

In chapter 1, I argued that preachers should begin their sermons like the writer of John began his Gospel: "In the beginning was the word." Preaching is the process by which the *written* Word (the biblical text) is employed to bring people into the presence of the *living* Word (Jesus

Christ) by the use of the *spoken* word (the sermon). This chapter has argued that the sermons we preach, which are designed to bring people into the presence of God, should be delivered with such passion and urgency that people are more likely to hear—and experience—the message we are declaring.

James Henry Harris describes this as "making the word plain." This is more than making the word simple for the mind to comprehend the "what" of the sermon. It has more to do with the "so what" of the sermon. He writes, "To make the Word plain is to interpret the Word in a way that speaks to the heart and soul of the parishioner. It means to interpret the biblical text and the congregation's context in a way that helps them to understand how to cope with the difficulties and joys of life."[13]

Both James Henry Harris and Evans Crawford[14] remind us that when sermons are being delivered in many black church settings, one can hear comments rising up from within the congregation as a kind of call and response between the pulpit and the pew. Utterances from the pews include, "Preach, preacher," "That's alright," "I hear you," and "Amen," among many others. In some liturgical contexts people may stand or raise their hands during the sermons. These are explicit vocal and kinesthetic expressions and signs that the hearers are emotionally engaged in the sermon, that the "so what" is becoming plain and meaningful to them. In some cultural contexts the emotional engagement is more internal and thus less demonstrative. This does not mean inviting the congregation to receive the word in a way that involves their heart as well as their head is any less important.

So how do preachers touch the hearts of the congregation? We have already spoken of the need for preachers to be passionate so that hearers will have corollary emotions, but they must also be intentional in terms of designing the sermon to accomplish one of two things; either to ignite or to invite specific emotional responses. To *ignite* an emotional response is to preach in a way that allows the message of the sermon to work like spontaneous combustion; creating that intense moment of understanding, illumination, conviction, or affirmation similar to the moment for Wesley when he said, "My heart felt strangely warmed."

On the other hand, to *invite* an emotional response is the intentional act of moving the listener beyond the immediacy of the feelings of the moment, and encouraging them to draw upon whatever emotions the sermon may have ignited to engage in some specific and appropriate next steps. The emotional response is not merely the feeling generated by the experience of hearing the sermon; it must also include some contextually appropriate way to respond to what has been said and heard. Some sermons can challenge people to call forth their untapped reservoirs of courage as they engage in a struggle for justice and social transformation. Other sermons can invite people to act upon their newly awakened sense of contrition and begin the quest for personal, spiritual transformation.

It must be restated that the responses that listeners are invited to make must be contextually appropriate. A funeral sermon and a revival sermon should not seek the same emotional engagement. The goal of a funeral eulogy is to ignite a flame of hope that can allow the listener to cope with the grief that surrounds them at that moment. The goal of a revival sermon is to invite the listeners to take a step either toward conversion, renewal, or recommitment to the cause of Christ and the work of the church. A sermon that invites people to take a stand on a social justice issue is different from a sermon that ignites people's awareness of the free gift of grace.

In short, it is the obligation of the preacher not only to have something to say but to say it in such a way that it moves the listeners to act upon the words they have just heard. In the next chapter, attention will be given to some of the specific emotional responses that can be generated when our sermons join together the passion that is demonstrated by the preacher and the passion that is created in the listeners. That will move this study from the first stage of the sermonic claim that is "What?" to the second stage that is "So what?" to the third and final stage that is "Now what?"

An Afterword on Patience

As difficult as it is to convey clear, understandable content to a congregation, it is even more difficult for a preacher to invite authentic, life-changing emotional involvement from hearers. It is much easier to lecture than to preach or to encourage surface-level emotionalism instead of true emotional depth. Beginning or aspiring preachers may wonder if they can ever match up to this level of preaching skill and competence.

It must be remembered that effectiveness or mastery in preaching, like effectiveness or mastery in any profession or in any art form, does not come easily, quickly, or automatically. The most highly skilled surgeons in the world began as medical residents and interns who were just learning the fundamentals of how to care for the human body. The most renowned musicians in the world began by practicing scales and learning music fundamentals. Mastery of any craft is, or should be, the goal of everyone engaged in that calling or vocation.

To reach the goal of effectively engaging hearers in the depths of their souls and transforming their lives, preachers must combine humility and hard work over the course of their career. In one of the many tributes following the death of the soul singer James Brown, an interview was aired that referred to this world-famous performer's first appearance on the stage of the famous Apollo Theater in New York City. Back then, the Apollo Theater was to soul music what the Grand Old Opry in Nashville was (and still is) to country music in America—the place where every aspiring soul singer in America knew they would have to win over the audience if they expected to go on and have a successful career. Brown recalled that when he first appeared at the Apollo in the early 1960s, he used a stage routine that had worked well in his hometown of Augusta, Georgia. However, it was not well received by that New York City audience whose approval and endorsement he wanted and needed. At one point in his performance, he threw some item of clothing into the audience as a souvenir. That gesture always worked well when he attempted it before other audiences in high school gyms and small social clubs across the country. When he did it in New York City, however, that item was thrown back onto the stage by someone who was unimpressed with Brown's performance. James Brown's first appearance on that "big stage" was less than impressive to that discriminating audience. In the taped interview that was shown following his death, Brown recalled saying to himself when he finished that first night at the Apollo Theater, "James, you have some work to do."

Between that first Apollo appearance and his death in 2006, James Brown did that work, and over the intervening forty years he appeared at the Apollo more times and before larger audiences than any other performer in the history of that famous theater. James Brown was not "The Godfather of Soul" or "The Hardest Working Man in Show

Business" when he started his career. However, as he worked at his craft and matured as a performer, he reached the pinnacle of success in his profession. His effectiveness as a performer and his mastery of the craft of showmanship was developed over time and through hard work.

The same thing that James Brown said to himself is what needs to be said to every aspiring and beginning preacher, even if it is difficult to hear: you have some work to do. You are not yet the preacher you are going to become, but you can become an effective preacher and you can gain mastery of your craft if you are willing to work hard at the techniques and fundamentals of preaching, and if you are willing to explore and develop your talents.

Beginning and aspiring preachers must develop sermons that have something significant to say to specific congregations at specific points in time. They must remember that anything worth saying is worth saying well, and that means "making it plain" or preaching with urgency and conviction in such a way that it invites a similar emotional response from the listeners. They must never forget that preaching is not about them; it is about God and God's people. People come to church to hear a word from the Lord, not an opinion or a clever comment from the preacher.

Do not try to rush the process of effective preaching. Your preaching voice evolves naturally as you mature both spiritually and intellectually. It evolves as you gain experience preaching in diverse settings and before diverse audiences. It evolves as you discover your own voice and your gifts and skills for public speaking. Your development as a preacher can be short-circuited if you become so enamored with the preaching style of others that you fail to discover your own capacities and strengths and confront your own weaknesses. I have often heard it said that when a young or beginning preacher imitates the style of another, more experienced preacher, the young preacher ends up failing twice. The first failure is because we cannot really be like anyone else since we do not have the benefit of their education, their experiences, and their endowments. The second failure, far more significant than the first, is that we fail to become that unique preacher that God called and equipped us to become.

While sitting in a dentist's chair one day I noticed a long list of quips and comments placed on the ceiling above me, undoubtedly placed there in hopes of distracting me from the drilling that was about to occur inside my mouth. It worked, because the whole time the dentist was working, my eye was fixed on one of those phrases on the ceiling that said, "Triumph is nothing more than try with an 'umph'." Good preaching works in just this way; it comes from people who try with an "umph." It was never meant to be easy, and effectiveness requires effort and dedication. However, if beginning preachers are willing to "try" with an "umph," or if they are willing to say with James Brown, "I have some work to do," effective preaching and/or mastery of the craft measured against the very highest standard is within their grasp.

Chapter 3

Now What?

Everyone then who hears these words of mine and acts on
them is like a wise man who built his house on rock. —Matt. 7:24

Ethos

We have referred to Aristotle's approaches to persuasive rhetoric as
one way to grasp what we mean by sermonic claim. *Logos* is the appeal
to the hearer's intellect; thus, one aspect of the claim is the theological
content of the sermon. *Pathos* is the appeal to the hearer's emotions.
In terms of preaching, the preacher's passion during the sermon hope-
fully invites the congregation into an emotional, existential experience
of the content being discussed. We now turn to Aristotle's third and
final approach: *ethos*. For Aristotle, *ethos* refers to the hearers being
persuaded by the speaker's character.[1] In this chapter, I want to extend
Aristotle's focus on the speaker's character to talk about how preaching participates in forming the character of those in the pews. *Ethos*
is the etymological root of ethics, and so we turn now to the kinds
of behavior preachers seek to instill in their listeners. Put differently,
we shift from discussing the "what" that preacher should be saying
and the "so what" the congregation should be feeling to the question,
"Now what?" Once the sermon has been preached, what does the
preacher expect the hearers to do with what they have just heard?

It could be argued that one third of the act of preaching involves
techniques and skills related to text selection and biblical exegesis

that allow the preacher to arrive at what is going to be said in the sermon. Another third of the preaching experience involves techniques of sermon design and sermon delivery that make the case for why the claim or theme or message of the sermon should actually be heard and considered by the listeners. The preacher alone controls these first two steps in the process, and those two aspects of the work should be approached with discipline, diligence, and determination to prepare the clearest and most compelling message possible. This is the work of the preacher in study, in preparation, and in prayer. After that, the preacher must facilitate the remaining third of the process, which resides primarily with the hearers. We may have an insightful and compelling idea to present in our sermon, but unless it is delivered in ways that appeal to listeners' minds, hearts, *and* behavior, not much will come as a result of our preaching.

Think of the most famous speeches that have ever been uttered and the same basic rule will apply: the use of eloquence was meant to appeal first to the ear and the mind and then to the heart, *so that* the hearers would be inspired to take action. Patrick Henry's words, "Give me liberty or give me death," were designed to encourage his hearers to follow his example and resist the continued rule of the Kingdom of Great Britain in the American colonies. Abraham Lincoln's words in his second inaugural address, "With charity toward all and with malice toward none," were meant to encourage the citizens of the Union to welcome former Confederate loyalists back into the unified country despite the horrors of the Civil War. When Martin Luther King Jr. said, "There comes a time when silence is betrayal," he was inviting all Americans to share in his decision to speak out against the ongoing war in Vietnam. When President John F. Kennedy said, "Ask not what your country can do for you, but what you can do for your country," he was calling upon an entire nation to assume an active role in the transformation of American society. How many times have we heard the evangelist Billy Graham end his sermon by calling upon the people in the arena or the stadium to "get up and come forward to receive Christ." From the streets and assemblies of ancient Greece to the political rhetoric and the evangelical revivals of twenty-first-century America, a model has emerged of how we as preachers should approach our work. The lessons on how to be effective communicators in this present day have been passed on to us by those who were among the very best communicators of previous generations.

Sermons could be compared to commencement services where things do not stop at the end of the program. They are actually just beginning. In a commencement ceremony graduates go forth to practice the skills and to apply the lessons imparted to them during their years of instruction. The time of learning has come to an end, but the time of making use of that learning in life's day-to-day situations is just beginning. There may even be a commencement speaker who will exhort and encourage the graduates to take what they have learned in school and use it to make the world a better place. The order of the day for a commencement ceremony is always the same: do something that will make good use (future) of what you have learned (past).

It is similar with preaching. The theological content and existential experience of the sermon should flow seamlessly into a challenge to the listeners to leave the setting where the sermon was preached and put the lessons learned from that sermon into some particular practice. One might even say that the sermon is not truly finished when the preacher stops speaking. The sermon is only truly finished when the hearers receive what has been said and begin to apply it to their lives. As Henry H. Mitchell has observed, every sermon ought to be preached with a behavioral outcome in mind. He urges preachers to choose biblical texts as the basis of their sermons that "supply or imply not only truths but a *behavioral goal* in the hearer. No truth is significant that has no obvious counterpart in human action or attitudes."[2] He elaborates on this assertion elsewhere:

> Second only to the scriptural text is the sermon's behavioral purpose. . . . the purpose should embody the action demanded by the biblical text, and it should reflect the preacher's "gut" motivation for writing the sermon. . . . The hearers are always the actors. The desired behavior may be for them to grow in forgiveness, honesty, unselfish service, or commitment to labor for peace or against world hunger. . . . The ultimate goal is not what the preacher will *say* about it but what they will *do* about it in their everyday lives.[3]

The Good News Hour

One of my favorite pastimes is watching the local and national news on television. Over the years it has occurred to me that there is one thing that differentiates preaching from reporting the news. For the TV news anchor, the act of offering the information is all that is expected. Consider the people who anchor the evening news programs on TV. They read to us off of a teleprompter and their goal is to inform us about current events. However, it is neither their goal nor their role to advise us on what actions we should take in response to what we have just heard them report. Walter Cronkite, the former CBS Evening News anchor, used to sign off with the statement, "That's the way it is." All we accept from news reporters are the facts, a supposedly objective description of the way things are. When the news program goes off, there is no expectation that listeners will recreate that famous scene in the movie *Network*, where a fictional reporter directs his viewers to stick their heads out of the windows of their homes and apartments and shout "I'm as mad as hell, and I'm not going to take this anymore!"[4] Instead, life will go on unchanged for most people who will respond to what they have heard with little more than a shake of the head or a shrug of the shoulder.

Something different happens in the commercial breaks during the news, however. Viewers are exposed to a series of fast-talking salespeople who are always trying to convince us to buy things we do not need with money we cannot afford to spend. They offer everything from new cars to "Golden Oldies" music to cutting-edge kitchen and cleaning products that "no home should be without." These commercials do not simply describe these products, they go on to suggest how much better one's life would be if you owned them or used them or at least learned more about them. The sales pitch does not end simply with the giving of information about whatever is being promoted or advertised. No commercial is complete until some action is suggested or some direction is given to the viewers. There are several next steps that can be heard every night during commercial breaks from the news; "Ask your doctor if this is right for you." "Pick up the phone and call right now." "Don't go another day without trying this product." "Stop using or driving or eating some old product, and start enjoying this new product right away." These ads and commercials are occasionally obnoxious and a bit pushy, and I don't want to push this analogy too far. In a capitalistic culture based upon buying and selling and no small amount of fraud and deception, I am not urging preachers to take on the persona of a used-car salesman. Any attempt to compare preaching to selling can be viewed as a crass cheapening of the divine office and as a step in the direction of distorting the essential truth of the biblical message. Nevertheless, sermons can be seen as similar to TV commercials in having a clear objective to convince the audience to take some specific, suggested action.

Better, the work of preaching is to fuse into a single presentation both the up-to-date content of the news anchor and the passionate call to take action that comes from the salesperson. We should help people look at the world as it is, focusing on issues of war, poverty, HIV/ AIDS, bigotry, skyrocketing gasoline prices, plummeting stock market results, and an endless stream of candidates for public office who do not seem to have any idea what life is really like for average Americans whose jobs are being downsized and outsourced and whose dreams are being deferred as their income is being flattened. "That's the way it is!" A record number of homes in America are in foreclosure as people struggle with the deceptive practices of subprime lenders, and in many of our nation's inner cities there are more payday loans than there are fast-food restaurants. "That's the way it is." Preachers should be willing to talk about the fundamental problems that confront their congregation, their community, and their country. "That's the way it is."

However, the preacher should also be prepared to offer some *good* news to the listeners, whether it takes the shape of an attitude or an action that can help them cope with the circumstances of their lives. "There is a God in whom we can trust during times like these; let's trust God." That is good news which should be preached with energy and enthusiasm. There are acts of caring and kindness we can display toward those whose needs are greater than our own; let's display that kindness. That sort of action stands at the heart of the gospel message (cf. Matt. 25:31-44), and we should lift it up with a clear sense of urgency: "There are steps each of us can take to preserve the creation made by God and entrusted to humanity; let's take those steps. There are attitudes and prejudices that we still possess that keep us from coming to the aid of certain groups of people; let's seek God's help in abandoning those attitudes and prejudices."

Biblical Models
Another way to get at the behavioral and attitudinal aspect of the sermonic claim is to consider Deuteronomy 6:4, which reads, "Hear,

O Israel: The Lord our God, the Lord is one. . . ." (NIV). This is a key passage in the First Testament and central to Jewish prayers still today. In Hebrew, the first word, usually translated as the imperative "hear," is *shema*. *Shema* carries a much deeper meaning than "hear" suggests. It does not simply mean "hear" in the sense of a sound being received by the ear. *Shema* also carries the sense that people should act on and be in compliance with what they have just heard, the concern that the spoken word is being acted upon and obeyed.

From the perspective of ancient Israel the word *shema* meant more than confessing that there is only one God or adopting monotheism as a theological principle. Instead, the goal and objective of the word *shema* was for the people to worship and serve only one God even though they existed in a polytheistic culture where neighboring nations worshiped many different gods. More importantly, it meant that the people of Israel should resist any and every impulse to recognize and turn to the gods of their neighbors instead of placing their hope and trust entirely in the God they called Yahweh. From a "now what" perspective, the issue is not simply being heard by the ear but rather in being heard and heeded by the heart in ways that result in compliance with what is being said.

God speaks to Israel in Deuteronomy 6:4 in a way that all parents and children understand. When a parent says to one of their children, "Did you hear me?" the question does not really revolve around whether or not the words spoken by the parent were received by the ears of the children. The real implication of a parent saying, "Did you hear me?" is whether or not the child has started to do what the parent just directed her or him to do. That is the urgency with which we should approach our preaching. We should preach in ways that allow people to sense that God is actually saying to them, "Do you hear me?" Just as Deuteronomy 6:4 was offering both information and direction about how Israel should relate to their God, so, too, must we who preach the gospel provide both information and direction about how people should respond to the sermons we preach. As Henry Mitchell says, "The ultimate goal is not what the preacher will say about it [the action the sermon calls for] but what [the listeners] will do about it in their everyday lives."[5]

Or, turning to another biblical example, preachers do well to consider Paul's approach when he preached before Festus, the Roman governor of Judea, and Agrippa, the Jewish king (Acts 26). When Paul speaks in his own defense in what is essentially a trial that could result in his release or his execution, he makes it clear what outcome he is seeking from those who hear his appeal. He speaks with such power and conviction that Festus declares, "You are out of your mind, Paul! Too much learning is driving you insane!" After assuring the governor that he is not crazy but that he is actually preaching "the sober truth," Paul then turns his attention to King Agrippa and says to him, "King Agrippa, do you believe the prophets? I know that you believe." The king responds to Paul by saying, "Are you so quickly persuading me to become a Christian?" Paul responds with his eye clearly on the desired next step or the "now what" phase of preaching: "Whether quickly or not, I pray to God that not only you, but also all who are listening to me today might become as I am—except for these chains" (Acts 26:29).

Preachers may fear being viewed as being a bit pushy when they suggest to their listeners that the proclamation of God's good news requires a response analogous to those expected in these examples. However, it is better to be perceived as being pushy than to preach a sermon that ends without offering the listeners some answer to the question, "Now what?" You may recall the mention of Richard Borden's classic book, *Public Speaking—As Listeners Like It!*, in the previous chapter, where we discussed the need to overcome the audience's "Ho Hum" at the opening of a speech. Borden also has advice for the end of a speech. He writes,

> In the conclusion of your speech, ask your audience for some specific action—some action response which it is within their power to give. Join! Contribute! Vote! Write! Telegraph! Buy! Boycott! Enlist! Investigate! Acquit! Convict! When you feel tempted to end your speech without such a request for action, remember the Chinese proverb of the Middle Ages: "To talk much and arrive nowhere is the same as climbing a tree to catch a fish."[6]

The "now what" steps that can be taken can be as wide ranging as the teachings of the Bible or the core doctrines of the church: Trust in God! Step out in faith! Confess your sins! Repent and be baptized! Share what you have with those who are in need! Spend more time in prayer and in Bible study! Love those who hate you! "Now what" steps could go on to include any number of suggested next steps that can allow people to put what they have just heard into action. Tithe a portion of your income! Volunteer your time at a hunger center or serve as a mentor to a struggling student! Share your faith with someone outside of the church! Reconsider your opposition to women serving in the ministry of your denomination or of your local church! I reiterate Borden's observation that we should "ask the audience for some specific action—some action response which it is within their power to give." No sermon is complete unless it addresses the questions, "What?," "So what?," and "Now what?"

There are two very distinct reasons why no action may follow once a sermon has been preached. On the one hand, it is often the case that nonaction by the listeners is the result of their refusal to do what the preacher and the sermon are suggesting. There might have been an important message that was delivered with passion and urgency that resulted in a clear call to action on the part of the listeners, but the call was simply rejected. That was the case with Jesus in Luke 18:18-25. Jesus talks to a rich young ruler who inquires about the way to inherit eternal life. After assuring Jesus that he had kept the commandments of Moses since the earliest days of his youth, Jesus sets one more requirement before that young man: "Sell all that you own and distribute the money to the poor, and you will have treasure in heaven; then come, follow me." There was no part of the message that the young man could not understand, and there was no mistaking the fact that Jesus was directing his words to the very question with which that young man was wrestling. The young man knew and felt exactly what the next step was that he was being asked to make. He simply was not willing to do so.

On the other hand, there are numerous instances where the listener does not take any action at the end of the sermon because no action, no next step, no "Now what?" is ever asked of them. Nonaction by the listeners because they are unwilling to do what is being asked of them in a sermon is entirely different from nonaction by the listeners because the preacher and the sermon offer no suggestions at all as to what the listeners should do with what they have heard. The sermon has not been fully shaped and the claim of the sermon has not been fully preached until the preacher has offered the congregation an invitation to *act* upon the content and the experience of the sermon. What is the action that the sermon is calling upon the listeners to take?

Where do they go from here? What is God calling upon them to do? What changes in their lives need to be made? By the time the sermon is over the preacher should have given some hint as to what the listeners should do, not simply what they should know.

What Responses Should Preachers Invite?

What is the range of actions from which preachers can choose as they suggest to listeners what they should do with the claims made in the sermon?

In the broadest terms the actions we desire from the congregations to which we preach must be morally and ethically defensible. We have to be certain that whatever we suggest is consistent with the demands of conscience and with the claims of the gospel. We cannot and we must not encourage people to do what is contrary to the teachings of Scripture, as far as our best understanding of the truth of any given passage is concerned. Not only would we be inviting them to be unethical, but we would be acting unethically ourselves.

To limit the actions we desire from the congregations in this way is not the same thing as saying that the actions we aim for must be legal. Certainly this will usually be the case, but there have been significant moments in history where preachers were called to encourage believers to break what were considered to be unjust laws. Civil disobedience has biblical precedents. It was against the law for Daniel to pray to the God of Israel, having been told that all prayers should be directed to Darius, the king of Persia. Daniel knew about that law, but he broke that law as a matter of conscience and allegiance to Yahweh. Esther knew it was against the law to enter into the presence of King Ahasuerus (Xerxes), also of Persia, but she was persuaded to do so by her uncle, Mordecai, in order to appeal to the king for the preservation of her people against the plot by Haman to exterminate the Jews. It was against the law for Christians in the days of the Roman Empire to refuse to burn incense as a way of acknowledging the divinity of the Caesars. Knowing the consequences of their actions, they continually defied that law and died either by fire, or at the hands of gladiators, or by the jaws of starving lions as they cried out, "Christ is Lord!"

Of course, there are more recent examples of people acting out their faith by defying the law. Neither slavery in the United States, apartheid in South Africa, nor British rule in colonial India would have ended if there had not been people who were willing to break what they believed to be an unjust law as part of their commitment to establishing a more just and equitable society. Martin Luther King Jr. was able to persuade people to undertake dangerous marches and demonstrations, knowing that some state court or local sheriff had already declared illegal the very actions he was suggesting.

The actions to which we call congregations are rooted in standards higher than those established by cultural or political powers. We are seeking to live out the reign of God, not the reign of human conformity.

Model A: Four Types of Behavioral Responses

We can be more specific than this broad claim of simply inviting actions that are moral and ethical by naming a range of appropriate next steps that can be employed. Different sermons lead to different actions. Two typologies of behavioral responses to sermons are suggested by Robert McCracken, the pastor who had the unenviable task of succeeding Harry Emerson Fosdick at Riverside Church in New York City, and Cleophus LaRue, a professor of preaching at Princeton Theological Seminary.

We begin with McCracken, who, in his book *The Making of the Sermon*, makes an observation about what next steps people can and should be urged to take after they have heard a sermon. He says, "One criticism directed not unfairly against a great deal of contemporary preaching is that though relevant and timely in its way, and sometimes well expressed and well delivered, little actually comes of it." He then goes on to say, "The trouble with much preaching is that it fails either to kindle the mind or to energize the will. It seldom disturbs the conscience or stirs the heart."[7]

In this passing comment McCracken mentions four sermonic outcomes that are worth pausing over. A lifetime of effective preaching can be built upon lessons that can be garnered from simply expanding upon these four sermon outcome ideas. While McCracken is offering a critique of much preaching, we will express the four items in more positive terms: *Sermons should (1) kindle the mind, (2) energize the will, (3) disturb the conscience, or (4) stir the heart.*

1. ***Kindle the mind.*** There are some occasions when the goal of the sermon is to invite people to think about or rethink some issue

that the listeners might not otherwise consider. There are issues where clear answers are not available because people of goodwill and of deep and sincere Christian faith stand on both sides of the topic. There are traditional ways of doing things that are being challenged as the world around us continues to undergo rapid change. New things are happening in science and technology that leave many people of faith rocking and reeling from the implications of those advances. Sometimes the preacher and the sermon might want to consider these kinds of issues from a faith perspective so that their listeners have a better understanding of those issues and events. When does life begin—at conception or at the moment of birth? Is homosexuality a matter of biological makeup or is it a behavioral choice? Do the wars in Iraq and Afghanistan fit the definition of a "just war," and if not, how should Christians respond as these wars stretch out and cost more and more in both dollars and human lives? Is America really "a Christian nation," and if it is, then what are the rights that should be guaranteed to the increasing number of non-Christian immigrants who are becoming U.S. citizens? What are the implications of Genesis 1:28 where God says, "Be fruitful and increase in number; fill the earth and subdue it" (NIV) at a time when overpopulation is draining away earth's natural resources, and when subduing the earth is believed by many to have more to do with exploiting natural resources rather than with working to preserve and prolong them?

There is no yes-or-no answer to any of these issues. Instead, there are facts to be marshaled, arguments to be made, and hard thinking that needs to be inspired within our listeners. Giving people the facts and the faith perspective on those facts so they can think as mature Christians is a good outcome for a sermon.

Sermons that are designed to kindle the mind can open the door to a process that can continue long after the sermon has been preached. The Sunday morning sermon could be followed by a question-and-answer session over coffee in the social hall. It could flow over into small groups of church members that meet at various times and in various places away from the church to give further consideration to what was said in the sermon. Sermons that are designed to kindle the mind can be discussed in subsequent Sunday school classes or during a midweek Bible study with the pastor and other clergy on hand to provide biblical and theological resources.

This is what Paul seems to have accomplished with his sermon in Athens as recorded in Acts 17:16-34. Paul preached about the true nature of religious faith and about his own faith in Jesus Christ that was sealed by Christ's resurrection from the dead. While some people who heard Paul dismissed his message out of hand, there were others who responded by saying, "We want to hear you again on this matter." Paul had piqued their curiosity and aroused their interest. The matter had not been resolved for those people, but their minds had been kindled. A new and somewhat controversial topic had been introduced, and by getting some people from within that crowd in Athens to think about what had been said was a victory in itself. In fact, kindling the mind is often the first step on the way to the other behavioral responses to a sermon.

2. ***Energize the will.*** As a counterpoint to those who are quite content to think about and debate back and forth over the controversial issues of our time but never take any concrete actions, it is useful to remember that there are some occasions when the time for thinking has passed and the time for taking action has arrived. Sometimes the goal of the preacher is to motivate people to stop talking about something as an end in itself and instead to do something about the matter at hand. To energize the will is to encourage and empower people to act on the things they believe in and not to sit quietly by while great issues are being resolved and while difficult choices are being made by others.

During the heat of the civil rights movement in the 1950s and 1960s, Martin Luther King Jr. often referred to something he called "the paralysis of analysis." By that he was referring to those people who were so caught up in thinking and talking about the implications of racial integration and about the possible effects of equal protection under the law, they never managed to take any concrete steps toward achieving either of those goals. Their minds may have been engaged, but they had not been sufficiently motivated to move from analysis to action.

Every pastor knows about people in the church who may be willing to think and even talk about certain critical issues, but they are not willing to take any action on those issues. They will come to the stewardship banquet where the tithing concept will be explained and where the obvious personal and congregational benefits of tithing will be examined. However, when the pledge card is passed around there are many persons who will not commit themselves. This is only one example of dozens of areas in church life where sermons may need to be designed in ways that will motivate people in the church to take the actions that are being suggested.

We know that Matthew 25:31-44 refers to visiting those in prison, but getting people involved in the prison ministry program may require energizing their will. The church should certainly be open as a hunger center, but getting church members to serve as volunteers who will prepare or pass out the food may require energizing the will. People may quickly understand that if they are feeding their physical body three times a day, while feeding the spiritual body with only one sermon per week, they will eventually experience spiritual malnutrition. It is not hard to kindle the mind on that topic. That is something that people might gladly be willing to listen to and think about. The challenge is to persuade them or motivate them to spend more time in prayer, or Bible study, or group devotions.

Energizing the will of the listeners as an intended outcome may be most needed when it comes to motivating Christians to move beyond their comfort zone of activity and attitudes and enter into areas of ministry and service they have shunned in the past. It may be required when churches are being called upon to embrace changes in polity or doctrine or leadership they had long resisted. It may be necessary if the goal of the sermon is to persuade people to open up their local church to be an HIV/AIDS testing and support center, and also to convince members of that church to volunteer some time to help with the maintenance of such a program. The preacher may want to attempt to energize the will of the listeners by preaching a sermon where the desired outcome is to go out and share one's faith, or write a letter to voice one's opposition to a public policy, or to be open to changes in the worship service brought on by increased racial, cultural, or generational diversity within the congregation. In all of the above cases, there may have been a time when kindling the mind was all that was initially being sought. It is often a wise course of action to allow people time to think about and reflect upon the actions that are being set before them. However, "the paralysis of analysis" can happen as often in the church as it does in the shaping of public policy. At some point, therefore, the preacher needs to preach in a way that motivates people to get on with the business at hand. Thus there are instances when the appropriate response to the "now what" question is an energized will that is ready to take the positive actions set forth in the text and called forth from the sermon.

The Bible is full of sermons where an action is suggested or implied. In Joshua 24:15, Joshua challenges the people of Israel to "choose this day whom you will serve." In 1 Kings 18:21, Elijah challenges the people to "stop limping between two opinions. If God be God then serve Him. . . ." (NIV). In Matthew 7:24, Jesus tells his congregation in Galilee that "Everyone who hears these words of mine and puts them into practice is like a wise man who built his house on the rock" (NIV). In 1 Corinthians 11:1, Paul tells the church in Corinth, "Follow my example as I follow the example of Christ" (NIV). In his Pentecost Day sermon in Acts 2:38, Peter urged his audience in Jerusalem to "Repent, and be baptized every one of you in the name of Jesus Christ so that your sins may be forgiven."

The image of the watchman found in Ezekiel 3:16-21 is a clear reminder of where the job of the preacher ends and where the responsibility of the listeners begins. God tells the prophet to warn the people of any approaching danger so they will have time to respond and save themselves. Once the alarm has been sounded and the direction has been given, it is up to the listeners as to whether or not they will take the direction that has been suggested by the watchman. As preachers, we cannot guarantee that people will accept or agree to the next steps that flow from our sermons. All we can do is set forward what the "now what" steps should be and motivate people to take them. This is the meaning of energizing the will.

3. **Disturb the conscience.** The third possible behavioral goal for our sermons is to challenge people to confront the sins in their lives, including the corporate sins in our society about which we are so often either silent, complicit, or both. Disturbing the conscience also involves preaching that is designed to challenge and condemn false doctrine and the people who either teach it or adhere to it. Either way, bad behavior or false doctrines, one of the tasks of the preacher is to disturb the conscience of those involved in such things. Preaching that aims to disturb the conscience is seldom welcomed by the hearers, but it is essential if people are going to develop fully as disciples of Jesus Christ. There are behaviors that we as disciples need

to abandon. There are attitudes that we as Christians must no longer display. Even after we have confessed our sins, been born again, undergone baptism, and started down the path of discipleship, there are still those instances when we stray from the straight path and sometimes even return to the old ways. The job of the preacher is to help people see themselves as they are and then call them to become all that God has in mind for their lives.

The Bible is full of characters who can be used for a sermon that is intended to disturb the conscience if we know how to make the best use of these characters in our preaching. James Sanders talks about studying biblical characters as *mirrors*, not *models*, of human conduct and behavior.[8] His point is that no biblical character, with the single exception of Jesus, is qualified to be such a model of behavior, because sooner or later all of them let us down as they display murderous violence (Moses), cowardly fear and deception (Abraham with Sarah and Pharaoh), hostility toward the church and staunch resistance to the message about Jesus (the apostle Paul in his pre-Damascus-Road behavior), or refusing to stand up for what one believes (Peter, who denies Jesus three times in the Garden of Gethsemane). Instead of using biblical characters as models of how we *should* live, Sanders suggests that we use them as mirrors of how we actually *do* live. The anger of Moses dwells within many of us. The fear and faithlessness of Abraham is common to us as well. It is likely that we, too, would have abandoned Jesus on that night in Gethsemane and many have denied him under similar circumstances. Romans 3:23 is the operative verse; "All have sinned and fall short of the glory of God." It should not be forgotten that in the Gospel of Mark, both John the Baptist and Jesus begin their first sermons with the same theological focus: *Repent!* That call to conscience is just as necessary in the twenty-first century as it was in the first century. Sanders's final point is crucial: namely, that "the same God who could use the sinful characters in the Bible can also use us once we turn from our wicked ways." The job of the preacher, the "now what" phase of the sermon under this approach, is to help people focus on the sins in their lives, suggest the changes that people need to make or the actions people need to take, and then urge them to take those actions.

This kind of preaching is not often heard these days, as preachers are rushing to offer prosperity theology or to preach smiley-faced sermons about positive thinking and successful living. It is not likely that the evils of our society will ever be addressed or resolved unless and until more preachers are willing to say that the "now what" step in the lives of many people is to repent of their sins. This seems to be what the author of 2 Timothy is speaking of when he says that the goal of preaching should be not only to correct and encourage but also "to rebuke" (2 Tim. 4:2; see also 3:16-17 and Titus 1:13).

Disturbing the conscience may result in having to endure hardship (see 2 Tim. 4:5). Such a thing may occur in the life of a preacher who is determined to speak a word of rebuke to the congregation, the community, or the society as a whole. Disturbing the conscience might result in more than some preachers are willing to face—an offended major donor, a disgruntled church lay leader, a sudden reduction in church attendance and/or weekly giving as people express their displeasure over the cutting edge of the sermon with their feet and with their wallets. However, as Peter Gomes states in his book *The Scandalous Gospel of Jesus*, "It is very difficult to preach the gospel as Jesus did without giving offense, and the world has been filled with people capable of being offended."[9] It may not be as well received by the congregation as those sermons that are designed to comfort and console them, but like a surgeon who lances a boil or cuts away cancerous tissue in order to restore a patient to health, a sermon that disturbs the conscience of those who hear it is good medicine for the soul.

There is an important caution that every preacher must heed before they head down this road of disturbing the conscience of their listeners, namely, that sin is not only a problem of the people in the pews. It is a problem for the preacher as well. We should not—indeed, we dare not—preach *at* people about their sins, acting as if we are somehow above the fray. Instead, we should preach about the sins that challenge and frustrate *all of us*. Paul leads all of us into confronting our sinful behaviors when he cries out in Romans 7:19-24:

> For I do not do the good I want, but the evil I do not want is what I do. Now if I do what I do not want, it is no longer I that do it, but sin that dwells within me.
>
> So I find it to be a law that when I want to do what is good, evil lies close at hand. For I delight in the law of God in my inmost self, but I see in my members another law at war with the law of my mind, making me captive

to the law of sin that dwells in my members. Wretched man that I am! Who will rescue me from this body of death?

As the nineteenth-century spiritual song says, "It ain't my mother, and it ain't my father, but it's me, oh Lord, standing in the need of prayer."

The accounts of misconduct among high-profile preachers—from Jimmy Swaggart, to Jim Bakker, to Ted Haggard, to the recent allegations of financial fraud that forced the resignation of Richard Roberts as president of Oral Roberts University—has placed a cloud of suspicion over the head of all clergy as people assume, "That's the way they are," or wonder what any one of us might be "up to." Things only got worse when U.S. Senator Charles Grassley of Iowa launched an investigation into the financial practices of some of America's most prominent televangelists, including Creflo Dollar, Eddie Long, Paula White, Kenneth Copeland, Benny Hinn, and Joyce Meyer.[10] The imagery may be stark, but the principle behind Paul's words in 1 Corinthians 9:27 is beneficial for all of us who would presume to preach to others about their moral and ethical conduct. Paul says, "I beat my body and make it my slave so that after I have preached to others, I myself will not be disqualified for the prize" (NIV).

4. *Stir the Heart.* There comes a time when the goal of the preacher is to deliver a sermon that uplifts the spirit, that encourages people in their striving to live faithfully, that restores their hope and equips them with perseverance in the face of some bleak forecast, or that allows people to celebrate the great things that God has done both in their lives and in the lives of others. Lamentations 3:21-23 is a wonderful verse with which to stir the heart, because it stands on the shoulders of the traumatic events that engulfed the people of Judah following the Babylonian conquest of their nation in 586 B.C.E. That passage states:

> Yet this I call to mind, and therefore I have hope,
> Because of the LORD's great love we are not consumed;
> For his compassions never fail.
> They are new every morning; great is your faithfulness. (NIV)

The rejoicing that occurs as a result of sermons based upon a text like this one is rooted in the love, mercy, and boundless provision of

God. There is no need to attempt the manipulation of the emotions of people by going through a series of timeworn devices that are sure to excite a crowd. The experience is all too common of listening to a preacher who has nothing substantive to say, and so relies instead on some emotional, manipulative device that may result in getting a congregation stirred up to a fever pitch. However, if most of those who heard such a sermon were to be approached only moments later and asked what the main theme of that sermon was, most would be unable to say anything more than "He/she really preached today."

Model B: Five Types of Behavioral Responses

Having considered the benefits of McCracken's four categories for answering the "now what" step in the process of shaping the claim of the sermon, attention will now be given to the approach of Cleophus LaRue found in his book, *The Heart of Black Preaching*.[11] LaRue's categories overlap significantly with McCracken's, so we need not repeat our commentary with the same depth of the previous section. However, the different typology is worth laying next to McCracken's. Writing from the unique perspective of the black church, LaRue offers insights that are beneficial to listeners and congregations in other settings as well. He suggests that preaching works best when it rotates through five domains of experience that reflect the breadth and depth of human life: (1) *personal piety*, (2) *care of the soul*, (3) *social justice*, (4) *corporate concerns*, and (5) *maintenance of the institutional church*.

1. **Personal Piety.** Some sermons should be devoted to matters of personal piety with the hope that people will adopt spiritual-formation practices that will result in their beginning a life of devotion. He suggests that the sermon outcome for sermons in this area would be an invitation to "prayer, personal discipline, moral conduct, and the maintenance of a right relationship with God."[12]

2. **Care of the Soul.** Other sermons should focus on care of the soul, by which he means the four traditional areas of pastoral care, which are healing, guiding, sustaining, and reconciling. In terms of possible sermon outcomes, LaRue states, "The function of sermons created out of reflection on this domain is to salve or heal the wounds and brokenness of life through some form of encouragement, exhortation, consolation, renewal, instruction, or admonishment."[13] The "now what" step would involve the preacher attempting to urge the listeners

to receive and embrace the healing and the help that has been made available by God as set forth in the sermon.

3. **Social Justice.** The third domain of experience for LaRue is preaching that focuses on the wide range of social justice issues such as discrimination, oppression, violence, and poverty. The desired goal or sermon outcome for such sermons is to motivate people to engage in such actions as can result in "constructive social change that brings about fair and just treatment in systems and structures that negatively impact all people. . . ."[14]

4. **Corporate Concerns.** By "corporate concerns" LaRue refers to actions that can result in improving community life for an entire group of people. For black people, who are his target audience, this means that the sermon outcome would include such things as challenging one's audience into action through "lifting ourselves from the welfare rolls, reducing black-on-black crime, and calls for educational excellence."[15] One can easily imagine such sermons being addressed to any constituent group that needs to act on its own behalf to improve its position in society.

5. **Maintenance of the Institutional Church.** Whereas LaRue's first two types of responses involve the individual and the next two involve groups beyond the church, the final domain of experience that can result in a "now what" action after a sermon deals with inner life of the church. There are many necessary things that must be done if a local church or a denominational body is going to survive, and sermons must be preached with an eye toward persuading and motivating people to accomplish those tasks. The desired outcomes from such sermons can include such things as responding to a call for financial and volunteer support for such ministry areas as "missions, evangelism, Christian education, benevolence, and upkeep of the physical plant."[16]

Balance

Different sermons—different "whats" and "so whats"—call for different behavioral responses. It is important for preachers to intentionally rotate the sermon outcomes they invite to maintain freshness and vitality in preaching to the same people week after week. Either McCracken's or LaRue's typologies (or a combination of the two) can be used to check our sermons over time to see if we are inviting a healthy range of actions. They challenge preachers to establish both a rhythm and a rotation in their preaching schedules that can be efficient for the preacher and edifying for the people who hear our sermons.

Some preachers might be inclined to focus almost exclusively on just one of these sermon outcomes to the detriment of the others. Some preachers might be inclined to limit their next steps only to "personal piety." Others might spend most of their time scolding the congregation in the name of "disturbing the conscience." I know many preachers who limit themselves almost entirely to the sermon outcome of stirring the heart. They may do so believing that it is either easier for them or perhaps even more profitable to them if they concentrate their efforts on making people feel emotionally uplifted, rather than trying to challenge their thinking, or motivating them in some area of Christian discipleship, confronting and seeking to correct their sinful behavior.

As we should preach about a wide variety of themes and topics (*what*) and offer a range of emotional experiences of the gospel (*so what*), we must also equip and empower people to take all of the necessary next steps (*now what*) that can result in their becoming mature Christians. This absence of a proper balance in preaching was apparent at a conference I attended in 2007 about prophetic preaching. Every speaker was urging pastors to devote every one of their sermons to the themes of economic justice, racial prejudice, anti-war activism, and environmental concerns (especially as it is manifested in the inner city through such things as lead-based paint and the location of garbage dumps and toxic-waste sites). All of these topics certainly deserve some attention over the course of a year's preaching, but pastors who preach to the same congregation week after week over the course of many years understand better than those who were speaking that day that there are a multitude of other themes and topics that must be addressed, just as there are a multitude of actions and responses that people must take in response to those sermons.

There are young people who need to be counseled and encouraged to avoid the dangers of premature exposure to sex and drugs. There are people whose marriages are in chaos and who need to be challenged to take the steps that can get them back on track. There are individuals and families struggling with being infected with or affected by HIV/AIDS, and they need to be encouraged toward lives with hope and dignity in the face of a disease for which there is no cure. There are people who are completely outside the faith and who do not accept the claims of the Christian gospel, and there are also people who are floating around the margins of the church but who have never fully embraced the concept of conversion, or new life in Christ, or what John 3:3 refers to as "being born from above." Over the course of time, and with some attention given to a system of text and topic selection that can help guarantee that this occurs, preachers need to address a variety of themes, each one of which is as important and urgent as the next, that encourage the listeners to take whatever might be the appropriate or suggested *now what* step.

How Many Points? Only One

In his 1977 Beecher Lectures on Preaching at Yale Divinity School, Gardner Taylor attempted to answer a question that has occurred to every preacher at one point or another: "How many points ought there be in a sermon?" His humorous but equally serious answer was, "At least one." I recall this quote at the end of the book because there is an important link between Taylor's answer about a sermon having at least one point and the question of how many claims a sermon should make. In this case, the answer is not "at least one." The better answer is "only one."

We have been discussing the intellectual, emotional, and behavioral appeal of the pulpit. These are not three different claims of the sermon but three aspects of the singularly focused sermonic claim. This is the difference between organization and outcome so far as the sermon is concerned. The sermon may consist of a traditional three-point form of argument, but those three points ought to be directing the listeners to a single, central claim. The sermon may involve a dialectical approach of thesis/antithesis/synthesis, but that form of argument should still result in some consideration of a single sermon claim. The sermon may employ a narrative, or biographical, or expository form, but preachers should exercise care in being sure that the sermon is only asking for one clear and compelling next step from the listeners. Remember the central thesis of this book:

> Every sermon needs to make *one* clear, compelling, biblically centered, and
> contextually relevant claim that sets some aspect of God's will and God's

word before some specific segment of God's people. This is done with the
hope that those people will be challenged, informed, corrected, or encouraged as a result of the word set before them that day.

There might be a temptation on the part of those who have considered the four steps of Robert McCracken or the five steps of Cleophus LaRue to ask their listeners to consider more than one *now what*
step for a sermon. It is even possible that the biblical text is pointing in
more than one possible direction so far as next steps are concerned.
For instance, a sermon that is designed primarily to kindle the mind
might also work if it were designed to energize the will; thus, either
thinking or acting could be the appropriate next step. A sermon that is
designed to stir the heart over the goodness of God could also be used
to disturb the conscience as hearers begin to compare the goodness
and faithfulness of God to their own lack of faithfulness.

Even though any given text or any given sermon *could* be considered from multiple perspectives, it *should* only be directed toward one.
It is important to remember that the task of shaping the claim of the
sermon is not only to determine *what will be said* in a sermon but also
to decide what of the available claims that could be made *will not be*
considered—at least not in that sermon. The words of Fred Craddock
that we noted earlier are worth repeating: "many texts hold a surplus
of meaning . . . but not everything can be said at once. To aim at nothing *(or at everything)* is to miss everything, but to be specific and clear
in one's presentation is to make direct contact with many whose ages,
circumstances, and apparent needs are widely divergent."[17]

Given the often unpredictable nature of the people who listen to
sermons, who often manage to hear or think they have heard things
not actually intended by our sermons, it is crucial that preachers deliver
sermons that offer a single, compelling, clearly focused message, that
invite a single emotional experience, that call for a single behavioral
outcome, a next step, or a *now what* in mind. When preachers ignore
this step in the process and fail to answer the "now what" question,
they run the risk of lumping their sermons in with the TV channels that
are quickly changed, the junk mail that is discarded, and the unwanted
or uninteresting e-mails that are deleted without being read.

That idea of having our sermons dismissed or ignored by our listeners may be what Robert McCracken had in mind when he said, "One

criticism directed not unfairly against a great deal of contemporary preaching is that though relevant and timely in its way, and sometimes well expressed and well delivered, little actually comes of it."[18] Paying close attention to this last step in the process of shaping the sermonic claim can help in avoiding this pitfall of preaching. Sermons that are clear about the essential message that is being presented (*logos*), the experiential/existential import of the message for the listener (*pathos*), and the appropriate next steps that are being requested of the listeners (*ethos*) have an excellent chance of being heard and heeded by the listeners.

Notes

Chapter 1 • What to Preach?

1. Aristotle, *Rhetoric and Poetics of Aristotle* (New York: Modern Library, 1954), 24–25.

2. Haddon Robinson, *Biblical Preaching: The Development and Delivery of Expository Messages* (Grand Rapids: Baker, 1980), 19.

3. Samuel D. Proctor, *The Certain Sound of the Trumpet: Crafting a Sermon of Authority* (Valley Forge: Judson, 1994), 93–94.

4. Thomas G. Long, *The Witness of Preaching* (Louisville: Westminster John Knox, 1989; 2d ed., 2005).

5. Fred B. Craddock, *Preaching* (Nashville: Abingdon, 1985), 155.

6. Ibid., 156.

7. Ernest Campbell, "A Lover's Quarrel with Preaching," in *What's the Matter with Preaching Today?*, ed. Mike Graves (Louisville: Westminster John Knox, 2004), 55.

8. Ibid. p. 55.

9. Harold T. Bryson, *Expository Preaching: The Art of Preaching Through a Book of the Bible* (Nashville: Broadman and Holman, 1995), p. 78.

10. Ibid, 79.

11. Hughes Oliphant Old, "Preaching by the Book: Using the *Lectio Continua* Approach in Sermon Planning," *Reformed Worship: Resources for Planning and Leading Worship* 8 (June 1988), http://www.reformedworship.org/magazine/article.cfm?article_id=164&id=8, accessed May 27, 2008.

12. Robert N. Bellah, *The Broken Covenant: American Civil Religion in a Time of Trial* (New York: Seabury, 1975); Mary Douglas and Steven M. Tipton, eds., *Religion and America: Spirituality in a Secular Age* (Boston: Beacon, 1982); Ernest Lee Tuveson, *Redeemer Nation: The Idea of America's Redeemer Role* (Chicago: University of Chicago Press, 1968).

13. Daniel Ellsberg, "The Posse in the Pulpit," *Time*, May 23, 2005, 32–33, cf. Marvin A. McMickle, "From Biblical Prophets to Patriot Pastors," in *Where Have All the Prophets Gone? Reclaiming Prophetic Preaching in America* (Cleveland: Pilgrim, 2006), 65–77.

14. "Worship as Higher Politics," *Christianity Today* (July 2005), 22.

15. In *New Proclamation Commentary on Feasts, Celebrations, and Other Celebrations*, ed. David B. Lott (Minneapolis: Fortress Press, 2007), Jennifer L. Lord

provides commentary on most of the days cited below, plus thoughts on preaching for the Week of Prayer for Christian Unity, Earth Day, a day of peace, and a harvest celebration.

16. C. H. Dodd, *The Apostolic Preaching and Its Developments: Three Lectures with an Eschatology and History* (New York: Harper & Row, 1964).

17. William J. Carl III, "Doctrine," in *Concise Encyclopedia of Preaching*, ed. William H. Willimon and Richard Lischer (Louisville: Westminster John Knox, 1995), 102; Ronald J. Allen, *Preaching Is Believing: The Sermon as Theological Reflection* (Louisville: Westminster John Knox, 2002); Burton Z. Cooper and John S. McClure, *Claiming Theology in the Pulpit* (Louisville: Westminster John Knox, 2003); and James F. Kay, *Preaching and Theology*, Preaching and Its Partners (St. Louis: Chalice, 2007). In the Elements of Preaching series, see Ronald J. Allen, *Thinking Theologically: The Preacher as Theologian* (Minneapolis: Fortress Press, 2008).

18. Robert White Jr., *Doctrine That Dances: Bringing Doctrinal Preaching and Teaching to Life* (Nashville: B&H Academic, 2008), 15.

19. Robinson, *Biblical Preaching*, 77.

20. There are several useful texts that can help preachers as they attempt to preach on some of the current events that are unfolding in the world today: McMickle, *Where Have All the Prophets Gone*; Tony Campolo, *Speaking My Mind: The Radical Evangelical Prophet Tackles the Tough Issues Christians Are Afraid to Face* (Nashville: W. Pub. Co., 2004); William Sloane Coffin, *A Passion for the Possible: A Message to U.S. Churches*, 2d ed. (Louisville: Westminster John Knox, 2004); Andre Resner Jr., ed., *Just Preaching: Prophetic Voices for Economic Justice* (St. Louis: Chalice, 2003).

21. Cleophus J. LaRue, *The Heart of Black Preaching* (Louisville: Westminster John Knox, 2000), 24–25.

22. Ibid., 25.

23. Thomas L. Friedman, *The World Is Flat: A Brief History of the Twenty-First Century* (New York: Farrar, Straus and Giroux, 2005).

24. See Mary F. Foskett, *Interpreting the Bible: Approaching the Text in Preparation for Preaching*, Elements of Preaching (Minneapolis: Fortress Press, forthcoming, 2009).

25. Marvin A. McMickle, *Living Water for Thirsty Souls: Unleashing the Power of Exegetical Preaching* (Valley Forge: Judson, 2001).

26. Joseph Stowell, interviewed in *Biblical Sermons: How Twelve Preachers Apply the Principles of Biblical Preaching*, ed. Haddon W. Robinson (Grand Rapids: Baker, 1989), 174.

27. Cf. pp. 6–7 in this chapter for a review of these approaches to shaping the claim of the sermon and why the use of a single sentence is so important.

28. Cf. p. 6 of this chapter for more on this definition.

29. Some include Robert Kysar and Joseph M. Webb, *Preaching to Postmoderns: New Perspectives for Proclaiming the Message* (Peabody: Hendrickson, 2006); Graham Johnston, *Preaching to a Postmodern World: A Guide to Reaching Twenty-first Century Listeners* (Grand Rapids: Baker, 2001); Ronald J. Allen, Barbara Shires Blaisdell, and Scott Black Johnston, *Theology for Preaching: Authority, Truth, and Knowledge of God in a Postmodern Ethos*

Chapter 2 • So What?

1. Richard Borden, *Public Speaking—As Listeners Like It!* (New York: Harper & Bros., 1935). I will discuss other items in the checklist in the following chapter.

2. Ibid, 4.

3. Ibid, 3.

4. Eugene L. Lowry, *The Homiletical Plot: The Sermon as Narrative Art Form* (Atlanta: John Knox, 1980), 20.

5. A. J. Jacobs, *The Year of Living Biblically: One Man's Humble Quest to Follow the Bible as Literally as Possible* (New York: Simon & Schuster, 2007).

6. Charles Chauncy, "Enthusiasm Described and Caution'd Against," in *The Great Awakening: Documents Illustrating the Crisis and Its Consequences*, ed. Alan Heimert and Perry Miller (New York: Macmillan, 1967), 230–31. We must be beware, however, agreeing with Chauncy uncritically; some of those he accused of emotionalism are the same ones Henry Mitchell lifted up as positive examples of the Great Awakening, mentioned above.

7. See Walter S. Thomas, *Good Meat Makes Its Own Gravy: 135 Servings for the Soul*, compiled and ed. Allison Elizabeth Brown (Valley Forge: Judson, 2000).

8. W. Floyd Breese, "Emotion in Preaching," *Ministry* (March 1984), 8.

9. Marvin A. McMickle, *Living Water for Thirsty Souls: Unleashing the Power of Exegetical Preaching* (Valley Forge: Judson, 2001), 185.

10. There is a wonderful treatment of the importance of emotion in preaching found in Evans E. Crawford and Thomas H. Troeger, *The Hum: Call and Response in African American Preaching* (Nashville: Abingdon, 1995), 21.

11. Henry H. Mitchell, "African American Preaching: The Future of a Rich Tradition," *Interpretation* (October 1997), 380–83.

12. Halford Luccock, *Communicating the Gospel* (New York: Harper & Bros., 1954), 145.

13. James Henry Harris, *The Word Made Plain: The Power and Promise of Preaching* (Minneapolis: Fortress Press, 2004), ix.

14. Ibid.; and Crawford and Troeger, *The Hum*, 21.

Chapter 3 • Now What?

1. Aristotle, *Rhetoric and Poetics of Aristotle* (New York: Modern Library, 1954), 24–25.

2. Henry H. Mitchell, "African American Preaching: The Future of a Rich Tradition," *Interpretation* (October 1997), 378.

3. Henry H. Mitchell, *Celebration and Experience in Preaching* (Nashville: Abingdon, 1990), 53–54.

4. Paddy Chayefsky, *Network*, directed by Sidney Lumet (MGM, 1977).

5. Mitchell, *Celebration and Experience in Preaching*, 54.

6. Richard Borden, *Public Speaking—As Listeners Like It!* (New York: Harper & Bros., 1935), 12–13.

7. Robert J. McCracken, *The Making of the Sermon* (New York: Harper & Bros., 1956), 18.

8. James A. Sanders, "Hermeneutics," in *The Interpreter's Dictionary of the Bible*, Supplementary Volume (Nashville: Abingdon, 1976), 406.

9. Peter Gomes, *The Scandalous Gospel of Jesus: What's So Good about the Good News?* (New York: Harper One, 2007), 20.

10. David Van Biema, "Going After the Money Ministries," *Time* (November 26, 2007), 51–52.

11. Cleophus J. LaRue, *The Heart of Black Preaching* (Louisville: Westminster John Knox, 2000), 21–25.

12. Ibid., 22.

13. Ibid.

14. Ibid., 23.

15. Ibid., 24.

16. Ibid.

17. Fred Craddock, *Preaching* (Nashville: Abingdon, 1985), 156; italics added.

18. McCracken, *The Making of the Sermon*, 18.

Representative Readings

Childers, Jana, ed. *Birthing the Sermon: Women Preachers on the Creative Process.* St. Louis: Chalice, 2001. This book is designed to answer one of the perennial questions for every preacher: "Where do preachers get their ideas for sermons, and how do they turn those ideas into great sermons week after week?" Twelve female preachers, six professors of homiletics, five pastors, and one rabbi speak to this issue. Each contributor offers both a brief essay on some aspect of sermon design and development, followed by a sample sermon in which the reader can see how the initial sermon has evolved into a finished sermon.

Fry Brown, Teresa L. *Weary Throats and New Songs.* Nashville: Abingdon, 2003. An insightful and instructive treatise on the historic struggle of women to gain recognition of their call to preach, and on the themes and topics that black women preachers have employed as they given expression to their faith. Brown not only offers valuable tips on sermon structure and delivery, but the book also contains several sample sermons in which you can see her preaching principles at work. The church can be blessed when it listens to all of the voices and all of the experiences that God has called to the preaching ministry. This book is just the tip of the iceberg of that blessing.

Graves, Mike, ed. *What's the Matter With Preaching Today?* Louisville: Westminster John Knox, 2004. Beyond the chapter offered by Ernest Campbell that has already been referred to in the present study, the other essays in this book allow some of the nation's top preachers and scholars of preaching to examine the state of preaching in contemporary America. Each writer is called upon to react to the 1928 essay by Harry Emerson Fosdick in which he raised the question, *What is the matter with preaching?* What each respondent does in turn is to offer some insights not only as it regards the challenges that confront those who are called upon to preach, but also some suggestions on how to make preaching more effective and authoritative in the twenty-first century.

Johnston, Robert K. *Reel Spirituality: Theology and Film in Dialogue.* Grand Rapids: Baker, 2000. Motion pictures have become a standard genre from which sermon ideas, topics, illustrations, and life applications are regularly being drawn. In some respects, filmmakers and preachers are competing for the same audience, even though they may not be telling the same story or exalting the same god. Johnston helps the preacher see not only the downside of the message of many contemporary films, but also the potential that exists for preachers to tap into film stories as a way to enrich the preaching of the gospel message whether through confirming or confronting what people hear and see in the films they view. Johnston reminds the church that a theological conversation is going on in homes and coffeehouses without any preacher as people discuss the films they have viewed together. With church attendance down and attendance at movies skyrocketing, preachers need to enter into the conversation about reel spirituality.

Kaiser, Walter C., Jr. *Revive Us Again: Biblical Insights for Encouraging Spiritual Renewal.* Nashville: Broadman & Holman, 1999. Here is a book by a biblical scholar which clearly understands that preaching must do a better job of generating spiritual renewal and revival within the hearts of those who hear our sermons. Given the tragic events of the last one hundred years, ranging from world wars, to the Holocaust, to the perceived decline of any shared moral values as a nation, Kaiser reminds us that effective biblical preaching can bring about a spiritual renewal in our lives, in our churches, and also in our nation. Preaching should always be done with some desired outcome in mind. For Kaiser that outcome is the spiritual renewal which preaching has fueled in earlier times in church history, and which solid biblical preaching can fuel once again.

Kysar, Robert, and Joseph M. Webb. *Preaching to Postmoderns: New Perspectives for Proclaiming the Message.* Peabody, Mass.: Hendrickson, 2006. This important book helps twenty-first-century preachers respond to the challenges of proclamation in what has widely been called the "postmodern" world. The book equips preachers to approach their work in a cultural context in which issues about the authority of Scripture, the acceptance of any spiritual path being as good as any other, and people's lack of familiarity with both biblical content and church jargon can make effective preaching difficult to achieve. The writers employ various approaches to biblical interpretation and textual analysis in order to unlock the valuable lessons the Bible has for our present world. Here is real help in how to approach the use of the Bible in preaching that can make the Scriptures accessible and authoritative.

LaRue, Cleophus, ed. *Power in the Pulpit: How America's Most Effective Black Preachers Prepare Their Sermons.* Louisville: Westminster John Knox, 2002. Here is an invaluable tool from an enviable list of some of today's best preachers. From veteran voices like Gardner Taylor and J. Alfred Smith, to several strong women preachers including Prathia Hall and Carolyn Knight, this collection of essays and sermons covers every topic from exegesis, to hermeneutics, to the development and delivery of sermons. This book reminds the reader that there is no single form that captures the essence of black preaching whether one considers content or form. This book really does offer twelve distinct approaches to the task of conceiving and shaping the sermon.

Massey, James Earl. *The Burdensome Joy of Preaching.* Nashville, Abingdon, 1998. Sermon preparation is a two-sided venture. On the one hand is what Massey calls the inward journey or the spiritual formation that must occur within anyone who wants to preach with conviction and certainty. On the other hand, Massey also calls for the outward journey, which involves careful attention being given to both the matter (content of the sermon) and the manner (anointing or charisma) of those who preach. Preaching for Massey is *burdensome* because of the rigorous preparation that is required if the task is to be done effectively. However, preaching is also a *joy* because of the redemptive effect a sermon can have in the lives of people on any given day.

McKinney, Lora Ellen. *View From the Pew: What Preachers Can Learn from Church Members.* Valley Forge: Judson, 2004. Preachers may tend to forget that their sermons are not just "delivered," they are also "received." How effective is our biblical interpretation? How relevant and helpful are our sermon themes and subjects? How can the preacher be sure that he/she is truly feeding the flock of God? This helpful book by a church deacon, the daughter of a distinguished preacher, and an established scholar in the field of church life and activity can help preachers remember that no matter what is on the preacher's mind, the pulpit can not afford to forget about the view from the pew.

Resner, Andre, Jr., ed. *Just Preaching: Prophetic Voices for Economic Justice.* St. Louis: Chalice, 2003. Part of the preacher's task is to address issues of social and economic justice, and this book is one of the best collections of essays and sermons available that is devoted to the single topic of God's demand for economic justice. This book forces the reader to consider such issues as child poverty, the dangers of "affluenza," the impact that military spending has on domestic programs dealing with the needs of the poorest in our nation, or the prophet's warning that God will judge us based upon how we show compassion for "the least of these." The Bible clearly speaks to God's concerns for the poor, the widow, the orphan, and the stranger among us. Here is a way to help preachers include those themes in their pulpit work.

Troeger, Thomas H. *Preaching and Worship*. St. Louis: Chalice, 2003. Most people think of preaching simply as a matter of the human voice. Troeger points out that good preaching and effective communication in the modern world demand that the preacher make use of the eye, ear, and body, as well as language and the meaning of words. Our whole being should be involved in our preaching, and our preaching should always be viewed as being only a part of the larger act of Christian worship. When preachers remember that they are being called upon to worship God with and through their sermons, and that they should do so with everything that is within me, the people who stand at the pulpit will be instantly inspired and the people who are seated in the pews will be greatly enriched.

Watkins, Ralph, with Jason A. Barr Jr., Jamal-Harrison Bryant, William Curtis, and Otis Moss III. *The Gospel Remix: Reaching the Hip Hop Generation*. Valley Forge: Judson, 2007. The emergence of hip-hop culture over the last twenty-five to thirty years has created both a cultural and a communications challenge for those who must preach to people, black and white, born since 1980. So many people who preach do so out of a worldview of the 1960s and the civil rights/Vietnam War era. Increasingly, the people to whom we preach or who we are trying to reach with our sermons see that era very nearly as ancient history. It is time for preachers to do again what they have had to do for two thousand years: make the gospel relevant for a new and different generation. A remix occurs when an old song is updated with new rhythms and some altered lyrics. Preachers from Paul to Martin Luther to John Wesley to Prathia Hall have attempted to "remix" the gospel so it could speak to their own time and place. This book helps preachers "remix" the message with the present generation of listeners in mind.